THE WORKS OF
MAX BEERBOHM

THE WORKS

OF

MAX BEERBOHM

with a bibliography by
JOHN LANE

ADELAIDE
MICHAEL WALMER
2013

The Works of Max Beerbohm first published 1896
©Max Beerbohm in the UK and Australia

This edition published 2013

by

Michael Walmer
49 Second Street
Gawler South
South Australia 5118

ISBN 978-0-9874835-7-7 paperback

' *Amid all he has here already achieved, full, we may*
think, of the quiet assurance of what is to come,
his attitude is still that of the scholar; he
seems still to be saying, before all
things, from first to last, " I
am utterly purposed
that I will not
offend." '

CONTENTS

DANDIES AND DANDIES

.

How very delightful Grego's drawings are ! For all their mad perspective and crude colour, they have indeed the sentiment of style, and they reveal, with surer delicacy than does any other record, the spirit of Mr. Brummell's day. Grego guides me, as Virgil Dante, through all the mysteries of that other world. He shows me those stiff-necked, over-hatted, wasp-waisted gentlemen, drinking Burgundy in the *Café des Milles Colonnes* or riding through the village of New-market upon their fat cobs or gambling at Crockford's. Grego's *Green Room of the Opera House* always delights me. The formal way in which Mdlle. Mercandotti is standing upon one leg for the pleasure of Lord Fife and Mr. Ball Hughes ; the grave regard directed by Lord Petersham towards that pretty little maid-a-mischief

3

who is risking her rouge beneath the chandelier ; the unbridled decorum of Mdlle. Hullin and the decorous debauchery of Prince Esterhazy in the distance, make altogether a quite enchanting picture. But, of the whole series, the most illuminative picture is certainly the *Ball at Almack's*. In the foreground stand two little figures, beneath whom, on the nether margin, are inscribed those splendid words, *Beau Brummell in Deep Conversation with the Duchess of Rutland*. The Duchess is a girl in pink, with a great wedge-comb erect among her ringlets, the Beau *très dégagé*, his head averse, his chin most supercilious upon his stock, one foot advanced, the gloved fingers of one hand caught lightly in his waistcoat ; in fact, the very deuce of a pose.

In this, as in all known images of the Beau, we are struck by the utter simplicity of his attire. The ' countless rings ' affected by D'Orsay, the many little golden chains, ' every one of them slighter than a cob-web,' that Disraeli loved to insinuate from one pocket to another of his vest, would have seemed vulgar to Mr. Brummell. For is it not to his fine scorn of accessories that we may trace that first aim of modern dandyism, the production of the supreme effect through

4

means the least extravagant ? In certain congruities of
dark cloth, in the rigid perfection of his linen, in the
symmetry of his glove with his hand, lay the secret of
Mr. Brummell's miracles. He was ever most economical, most scrupulous of means.   Treatment was
everything with him.   Even foolish Grace and foolish
Philip Wharton, in their book about the beaux and wits
of this period, speak of his dressing-room as 'a studio in
which he daily composed that elaborate portrait of
himself which was to be exhibited for a few hours in
the clubrooms of the town.' Mr. Brummell was,
indeed, in the utmost sense of the word, an artist.
No poet nor cook nor sculptor, ever bore that title
more worthily than he.

And really, outside his art, Mr. Brummell had a personality of almost Balzacian insignificance.   There have
been dandies, like D'Orsay, who were nearly painters ;
painters, like Mr. Whistler, who wished to be dandies ;
dandies, like Disraeli, who afterwards followed some
less arduous calling. I fancy Mr. Brummell was a
dandy, nothing but a dandy, from his cradle to that
fearful day when he lost his figure and had to flee the
country, even to that distant day when he died, a
broken exile, in the arms of two *religieuses*. At Eton,

5

no boy was so successful as he in avoiding that strict alternative of study and athletics which we force upon our youth. He once terrified a master, named Parker, by asserting that he thought cricket 'foolish.' Another time, after listening to a reprimand from the head-master, he twitted that learned man with the assymmetry of his neckcloth. Even in Oriel he could see little charm, and was glad to leave it, at the end of his first year, for a commission in the Tenth Hussars. Crack though the regiment was—indeed, all the commissions were granted by the Regent himself—young Mr. Brummell could not bear to see all his brother-officers in clothes exactly like his own ; was quite as deeply annoyed as would be some god, suddenly entering a restaurant of many mirrors. One day, he rode upon parade in a pale blue tunic, with silver epaulettes. The Colonel, apologising for the narrow system which compelled him to so painful a duty, asked him to leave the parade. The Beau saluted, trotted back to quarters and, that afternoon, sent in his papers. Henceforth he lived freely as a fop, in his maturity, should.

His *début* in the town was brilliant and delightful. Tales of his elegance had won for him there a precedent fame. He was reputed rich. It was known

that the Regent desired his acquaintance. And thus,
Fortune speeding the wheels of his cabriolet and
Fashion running to meet him with smiles and roses
in St. James's, he might well, had he been worldly or
a weakling, have yielded his soul to the polite follies.
But he passed them by. Once he was settled in his
suite, he never really strayed from his toilet-table, save
for a few brief hours. Thrice every day of the year
did he dress, and three hours were the average of his
every toilet, and other hours were spent in council
with the cutter of his coats or with the custodian of
his wardrobe. A single, devoted life! To White's,
to routs, to races, he went, it is true, not reluctantly.
He was known to have played battledore and shuttle-
cock in a moonlit garden with Mr. Previté and some
other gentlemen. His elopement with a young
Countess from a ball at Lady Jersey's was quite
notorious. It was even whispered that he once, in
the company of some friends, made as though he
would wrench the knocker off the door of some shop.
But these things he did, not, most certainly, for any
exuberant love of life. Rather did he regard them as
healthful exercise of the body and a charm against
that dreaded corpulency which, in the end, caused his

7

downfall. Some recreation from his work even the most strenuous artist must have ; and Mr. Brummell naturally sought his in that exalted sphere whose modish elegance accorded best with his temperament, the sphere of *le plus beau monde*. General Bucknall used to growl, from the window of the Guards' Club, that such a fellow was only fit to associate with tailors. But that was an old soldier's fallacy. The proper associates of an artist are they who practise his own art rather than they who—however honourably—do but cater for its practice. For the rest, I am sure that Mr. Brummell was no lackey, as they have suggested. He wished merely to be seen by those who were best qualified to appreciate the splendour of his achievements. Shall not the painter show his work in galleries, the poet flit down Paternoster Row ? Of rank, for its own sake, Mr. Brummell had no love. He patronised all his patrons. Even to the Regent his attitude was always that of a master in an art to one who is sincerely willing and anxious to learn from him.

Indeed, English society is always ruled by a dandy, and the more absolutely ruled the greater that dandy be. For dandyism, the perfect flower of outward

8

elegance, is the ideal it is always striving to realise in its own rather incoherent way. But there is no reason why dandyism should be confused, as it has been by nearly all writers, with mere social life. Its contact with social life is, indeed, but one of the accidents of an art. Its influence, like the scent of a flower, is diffused unconsciously. It has its own aims and laws, and knows none other. And the only person who ever fully acknowledged this truth in æsthetics is, of all persons most unlikely, the author of *Sartor Resartus*. That any one who dressed so very badly as did Thomas Carlyle should have tried to construct a philosophy of clothes has always seemed to me one of the most pathetic things in literature. He in the Temple of Vestments! Why sought he to intrude, another Clodius, upon those mysteries and light his pipe from those ardent censers? What were his hobnails that they should mar the pavement of that delicate Temple? Yet, for that he betrayed one secret rightly heard there, will I pardon his sacrilege. 'A dandy,' he cried through the mask of Teufelsdröck, 'is a clothes-wearing man, a man whose trade, office, and existence consists in the wearing of clothes. Every faculty of his soul, spirit, purse, and person is heroically conse-

9

crated to this one object, the wearing of clothes wisely and well.' Those are true words. They are, perhaps, the only true words in *Sartor Resartus*. And I speak with some authority. For I found the key to that empty book, long ago, in the lock of the author's empty wardrobe His hat, that is still preserved in Chelsea, formed an important clue.

But (behold !) as we repeat the true words of Teufelsdröck, there comes Monsieur Barbey D'Aurevilly, that gentle *moqueur*, drawling, with a wave of his hand, ' *Les esprits qui ne voient pas les choses que par leur plus petit côté, ont imaginé que le Dandysme était surtout l'art de la mise, une heureuse et audacieuse dictature en fait de toilette et d'élégance extérieure. Très-certainement c'est cela aussi, mais c'est bien davantage. Le Dandysme est toute une manière d'être et l'on n'est pas que par la côté matériellement visible. C'est une manière d'être entièrement composée de nuances, comme il arrive toujours dans les sociétés très-vieilles et très-civilisées.*' It is a pleasure to argue with so suave a subtlist, and we say to him that this comprehensive definition does not please us. We say we think he errs.

Not that Monsieur's analysis of the dandiacal mind is worthless by any means. Nor, when he declares

10

that George Brummell was the supreme king of the dandies and *fut le dandysme même*, can I but piously lay one hand upon the brim of my hat, the other upon my heart. But it is as an artist, and for his supremacy in the art of costume, and for all he did to gain the recognition of costume as in itself an art, and for that superb taste and subtle simplicity of mode whereby he was able to expel, at length, the Byzantine spirit of exuberance which had possessed St. James's and wherefore he is justly called the Father of Modern Costume, that I do most deeply revere him. It is not a little strange that Monsieur D'Aurevilly, the biographer who, in many ways, does seem most perfectly to have understood Mr. Brummell, should belittle to a mere phase that which was indeed the very core of his existence. To analyse the temperament of a great artist and then to declare that his art was but a part— a little part—of his temperament, is a foolish proceeding. It is as though a man should say that he finds, on analysis, that gunpowder is composed of potassium chloride (let me say), nitrate and power of explosion. Dandyism is ever the outcome of a carefully cultivated temperament, not part of the temperament itself. That *manière d'être, entièrement composée de nuances,* was not more, as the writer seems to have supposed, than attributory to Mr. Brummell's art. Nor is it even peculiar to dandies. All delicate spirits, to whatever art they turn, even if they turn to no art, assume an oblique attitude towards life. Of all dandies, Mr. Brummell did most steadfastly maintain this attitude. Like the single-minded artist that he was, he turned full and square towards his art and looked life straight in the face out of the corners of his eyes.

It is not hard to see how, in the effort to give Mr. Brummell his due place in history, Monsieur D'Aurevilly came to grief. It is but strange that he should have fallen into a rather obvious trap. Surely he should have perceived that, so long as Civilisation compels her children to wear clothes, the thoughtless multitude will never acknowledge dandyism to be an art. If considerations of modesty or hygiene compelled every one to stain canvas or chip marble every morning, painting and sculpture would in like manner be despised. Now, as these considerations do compel every one to envelop himself in things made of cloth and linen, this common duty is confounded with that fair procedure, elaborate of many thoughts, in whose accord the fop accomplishes his toilet, each morning afresh, Aurora speeding

on to gild his mirror. Not until nudity be popular will
the art of costume be really acknowledged. Nor even
then will it be approved. Communities are ever jealous
(quite naturally) of the artist who works for his own
pleasure, not for theirs—more jealous by far of him
whose energy is spent only upon the glorification of
himself alone. Carlyle speaks of dandyism as a survival
of ' the primeval superstition, self-worship.' ' *La vanité*,'
are almost the first words of Monsieur D'Aurevilly,
' *c'est un sentiment contre lequel tout le monde est impitoy-
able*.' Few remember that the dandy's vanity is far
different from the crude conceit of the merely handsome man. Dandyism is, after all, one of the decorative
arts. A fine ground to work upon is its first postulate.
And the dandy cares for his physical endowments only
in so far as they are susceptible of fine results. They
are just so much to him as to the decorative artist is
inilluminate parchment, the form of a white vase or
the surface of a wall where frescoes shall be.

Consider the words of Count D'Orsay, spoken on
the eve of some duel, ' We are not fairly matched. If
I were to wound him in the face it would not matter;
but if he were to wound me, *ce serait vraiment dom-
mage !* ' There we have a pure example of a dandy's

13

peculiar vanity—'It would be a real pity!' They
say that D'Orsay killed his man—no matter whom—in
this duel. He never should have gone out. Beau
Brummell never risked his dandyhood in these mean
encounters. But D'Orsay was a wayward, excessive
creature, too fond of life and other follies to achieve
real greatness. The power of his predecessor, the
Father of Modern Costume, is over us yet. All that
is left of D'Orsay's art is a waistcoat and a handful of
rings—vain relics of no more value for us than the
fiddle of Paganini or the mask of Menischus! I think
that in Carolo's painting of him, we can see the strength,
that was the weakness, of *le jeune Cupidon*. His fingers
are closed upon his cane as upon a sword. There is
mockery in the inconstant eyes. And the lips, so used
to close upon the wine-cup, in laughter so often parted,
they do not seem immobile, even now. Sad that one
so prodigally endowed as he was, with the three essen-
tials of a dandy—physical distinction, a sense of beauty
and wealth or, if you prefer the term, credit—should
not have done greater things. Much of his costume
was merely showy or eccentric, without the rotund
unity of the perfect fop's. It had been well had he
lacked that dash and spontaneous gallantry that make

him cut, it may be, a more attractive figure than Beau Brummell. The youth of St. James's gave him a wonderful welcome. The flight of Mr. Brummell had left them as sheep without a shepherd. They had even cried out against the inscrutable decrees of fashion and curtailed the height of their stocks. And (lo !) here, ambling down the Mall with tasselled cane, laughing in the window at White's or in Fop's Alley posturing, here, with the devil in his eyes and all the graces at his elbow, was D'Orsay, the prince paramount who should dominate London and should guard life from monotony by the daring of his whims. He accepted so many engagements that he often dressed very quickly both in the morning and at nightfall. His brilliant genius would sometimes enable him to appear faultless, but at other times not even his fine figure could quite dispel the shadow of a toilet too hastily conceived. Before long he took that fatal step, his marriage with Lady Harriet Gardiner. The marriage, as we all know, was not a happy one, though the wedding was very pretty. It ruined the life of Lady Harriet and of her mother, the Blessington. It won the poor Count further still further from his art and sent him spinning here, there, and everywhere. He was continually at Cleveden, or

Belvoir, or Welbeck, laughing gaily as he brought down our English partridges, or at Crockford's, smiling as he swept up our English guineas from the board. Holker declares that, excepting Mr. Turner, he was the finest equestrian in London and describes how the mob would gather every morning round his door to see him descend, insolent from his toilet, and mount and ride away. Indeed, he surpassed us all in all the exercises of the body. He even essayed preëminence in the arts (as if his own art were insufficient to his vitality !) and was for ever penning impenuous verses for circulation among his friends. There was no great harm in this, perhaps. Even the handwriting of Mr. Brummell was not unknown in the albums. But D'Orsay's painting of portraits is inexcusable. The æsthetic vision of a dandy should be bounded by his own mirror. A few crayon sketches of himself—*dilectissimæ imagines*—are as much as he should ever do. That D'Orsay's portraits, even his much-approved portrait of the Duke of Wellington, are quite amateurish, is no excuse. It is the process of painting which is repellent ; to force from little tubes of lead a glutinous flamboyance and to defile, with the hair of a camel therein steeped, taut canvas, is hardly the diversion for a gentleman ; and to have done all this for a man who was admittedly a field-marshal. . .

I have often thought that this selfish concentration, which is a part of dandyism, is also a symbol of that *einsamkeit* felt in greater or less degree by the practitioners of every art. But, curiously enough, the very unity of his mind with the ground he works on exposes the dandy to the influence of the world. In one way dandyism is the least selfish of all the arts. Musicians are seen and, except for a price, not heard. Only for a price may you read what poets have written. All painters are not so generous as Mr. Watts. But the dandy presents himself to the nation whenever he sallies from his front door. Princes and peasants alike may gaze upon his masterpieces. Now, any· art which is pursued directly under the eye of the public is always far more amenable to fashion than is an art with which the public is but vicariously concerned. Those standards to which artists have gradually accustomed it the public will not see lightly set at naught. Very rigid, for example, are the traditions of the theatre. If my brother were to declaim his lines at the Haymarket in the florotund manner of Macready, what a row there would be in the gallery ! It is only

by the impalpable process of evolution that change
comes to the theatre. Likewise in the sphere of
costume no swift rebellion can succeed, as was exem-
plified by the Prince's effort to revive knee-breeches.
Had his Royal Highness elected, in his wisdom, to
wear tight trousers strapped under his boots, 'smalls'
might, in their turn, have reappeared, and at length—
who knows ?—knee-breeches. It is only by the trifling
addition or elimination, modification or extension, made
by this or that dandy and copied by the rest, that the
mode proceeds. The young dandy will find certain
laws to which he must conform. If he outrage them
he will be hooted by the urchins of the street, not
unjustly, for he will have outraged the slowly con-
structed laws of artists who have preceded him. Let'
him reflect that fashion is no bondage imposed by alien
hands, but the last wisdom of his own kind, and that
true dandyism is the result of an artistic temperament
working upon a fine body within the wide limits of
fashion. Through this habit of conformity, which it
inculcates, the army has given us nearly all our finest
dandies, from Alcibiades to Colonel Br*b*z*n *de nos
jours*. Even Mr. Brummell, though he defied his
Colonel, must have owed some of his success to the

military spirit. Any parent intending his son to be a dandy will do well to send him first into the army, there to learn humility, as did his archetype, Apollo, in the house of Admetus. A sojourn at one of the Public Schools is also to be commended. The University it were well to avoid.

Of course, the dandy, like any other artist, has moments when his own period, palling, inclines him to antique modes. A fellow-student once told me that, after a long vacation spent in touch with modern life, he had hammered at the little gate of Merton and felt of a sudden his hat assume plumes and an expansive curl, the impress of a ruff about his neck, the dangle of a cloak and a sword. I, too, have my Elizabethan, my Caroline moments. I have gone to bed Georgian and awoken Early Victorian. Even savagery has charmed me. And at such times I have often wished I could find in my wardrobe suitable costumes. But these modish regrets are sterile, after all, and comprimend. What boots it to defy the conventions of our time ? The dandy is the 'child of his age,' and his best work must be produced in accord with the age's natural influence. The true dandy must always love contemporary costume. In this age, as in all

19

precedent ages, it is only the tasteless who cavil, being
impotent to win from it fair results. How futile their
voices are! The costume of the nineteenth century,
as shadowed for us first by Mr. Brummell, so quiet,
so reasonable, and, I say emphatically, so beautiful;
free from folly or affectation, yet susceptible to exquisite ordering; plastic, austere, economical, may not be
ignored. I spoke of the doom of swift rebellions, but I
doubt even if any soever gradual evolution will lead us
astray from the general precepts of Mr. Brummell's code.
At every step in the progress of democracy those precepts
will be strengthened. Every day their fashion is more
secure, corroborate. They are acknowledged by the
world. The barbarous costumes that in bygone days
were designed by class-hatred, or hatred of race, are
dying, very surely dying. The costermonger with his
pearl-emblazoned coat has been driven even from that
Variety Stage, whereon he sought a desperate sanctuary.
The clinquant corslet of the Swiss girl just survives at
bals costumés. I am told that the kilt is now confined
entirely to certain of the soldiery and to a small cult
of Scotch Archaïcists. I have seen men flock from
the boulevards of one capital and from the avenues of
another to be clad in Conduit Street. Even into

Oxford, that curious little city, where nothing is ever born nor anything ever quite dies, the force of the movement has penetrated, insomuch that tasselled cap and gown of degree are rarely seen in the streets or colleges. In a place which was until recent times scarcely less remote, Japan, the white and scarlet gardens are trod by men who are shod in boots like our own, who walk—rather strangely still—in close-cut cloth of little colour, and stop each other from time to time, laughing to show how that they too can furl an umbrella after the manner of real Europeans.

It is very nice, this universal acquiescence in the dress we have designed, but, if we reflect, not wonderful. There are three apparent reasons, and one of them is æsthetic. So to clothe the body that its fineness be revealed and its meanness veiled has been the æsthetic aim of all costume, but before our time the mean had never been struck. The ancient Romans went too far. Muffled in the ponderous folds of a toga, Adonis might pass for Punchinello, Punchinello for Adonis. The ancient Britons, on the other hand, did not go far enough. And so it had been in all ages down to that bright morning when Mr. Brummell, at his mirror, conceived the notion of

trousers and simple coats. Clad according to his convention, the limbs of the weakling escape contempt,
and the athlete is unobtrusive, and all is well. But
there is also a social reason for the triumph of our costume—the reason of economy. That austerity, which
has rejected from its toilet silk and velvet and all but
a few jewels, has made more ample the wardrobes of
Dives, and sent forth Irus nicely dressed among his
fellows. And lastly there is a reason of psychology,
most potent of all, perhaps. Is not the costume of to-
day, with its subtlety and sombre restraint, its quiet
congruities of black and white and grey, supremely apt
a medium for the expression of modern emotion and
modern thought? That aptness, even alone, would
explain its triumph. Let us be glad that we have so
easy, yet so delicate, a mode of expression.

Yes! costume, dandiacal or not, is in the highest
degree expressive, nor is there any type it may not
express. It enables us to classify any ' professional
man ' at a glance, be he lawyer, leech or what not.
Still more swift and obvious is its revelation of the
work and the soul of those who dress, whether naturally
or for effect, without reference to convention. The
bowler of Mr. Jerome K. Jerome is a perfect preface

to all his works. The silk hat of Mr. Whistler is a
real *nocturne*, his linen a symphony *en blanc majeur*. To
have seen Mr. Hall Caine is to have read his soul. His
flowing, formless cloak is as one of his own novels,
twenty-five editions latent in the folds of it. Melo-
drama crouches upon the brim of his *sombrero*. His tie
is a Publisher's Announcement. His boots are Copy-
right. In his hand he holds the staff of *The Family
Herald*.

But the dandy, innowise violating the laws of
fashion, can make more subtle symbols of his personality. More subtle these symbols are for the very
reason that they are effected within the restrictions
which are essential to an art. Chastened of all flamboyance, they are from most men occult, obvious, it
may be, only to other artists or even only to him they
symbolise. Nor will the dandy express merely a crude
idea of his personality, as does, for example, Mr. Hall
Caine, dressing himself always and exactly after one
pattern. Every day as his mood has changed since his
last toilet, he will vary the colour, texture, form of his
costume. Fashion does not rob him of free will. It
leaves him liberty of all expression. Every day there
is not one accessory, from the butterfly that alights

23

above his shirt front to the jewels planted in his linen, that will not symbolise the mood that is in him or the occasion of the coming day.

On this, the psychological side of foppery, I know not one so expert as him whom, not greatly caring for contemporary names, I will call Mr. Le V. No hero-worshipper am I, but I cannot write without enthusiasm of his simple life. He has not spurred his mind to the quest of shadows nor vexed his soul in the worship of any gods. No woman has wounded his heart, though he has gazed gallantly into the eyes of many women, intent, I fancy, upon his own miniature there. Nor is the incomparable set of his trousers spoilt by the perching of any dear little child upon his knee. And so, now that he is stricken with seventy years, he knows none of the bitterness of eld, for his toilet-table is an imperishable altar, his wardrobe a quiet nursery and very constant harem. Mr. Le V. has many disciples, young men who look to him for guidance in all that concerns costume, and each morning come, themselves tentatively clad, to watch the perfect procedure of his toilet and learn invaluable lessons. I myself, a lie-a-bed, often steal out, foregoing the best hours of the day abed, that I may attend that *levée*. The rooms of the

Master are in St. James's Street, and perhaps it were
well that I should give some little record of them and
of the manner of their use. In the first room the
Master sleeps. He is called by one of his valets, at
seven o'clock, to the second room, where he bathes, is
shampooed, is manicured and, at length, is enveloped
in a dressing-gown of white wool. In the third room
is his breakfast upon a little table and his letters and
some newspapers. Leisurely he sips his chocolate,
leisurely learns all that need be known. With a
cigarette he allows his temper, as informed by the news
and the weather and what not, to develop itself for the
day. At length, his mood suggests, imperceptibly,
what colour, what form of clothes he shall wear. He
rings for his valet—' I will wear such and such a coat,
such and such a tie ; my trousers shall be of this or
that tone ; this or that jewel shall be radiant in the
folds of my tie.' It is generally near noon that he
reaches the fourth room, the dressing-room. The
uninitiate can hardly realise how impressive is the
ceremonial there enacted. As I write, I can see, in
memory, the whole scene—the room, severely simple,
with its lemon walls and deep wardrobes of white
wood, the young fops, φιλομαθέστατοι τινες τῶν νεανίσκων,

ranged upon a long bench, rapt in wonder, and, in the middle, now sitting, now standing, negligently, before a long mirror, with a valet at either elbow, Mr. Le V., our cynosure. There is no haste, no faltering, when once the scheme of the day's toilet has been set. It is a calm toilet. A flower does not grow more calmly.

Any of us, any day, may see the gracious figure of Mr. Le V., as he saunters down the slope of St. James's. Long may the sun irradiate the surface of his tilted hat ! It is comfortable to know that, though he die to-morrow, the world will not lack a most elaborate record of his foppery. All his life he has kept or, rather, the current valets have kept for him, a *Journal de Toilette*. Of this there are now fifty volumes, each covering the space of a year. Yes, fifty springs have filled his button-hole with their violets ; the snow of fifty winters has been less white than his linen ; his boots have outshone fifty sequences of summer suns, and the colours of all those autumns have faded in the dry light of his apparel. The first page of each volume of the *Journal de Toilette* bears the signature of Mr. Le V. and of his two valets. Of the other pages each is given up, as in other diaries, to one day of the year. In ruled spaces

26

are recorded there the cut and texture of the suit, the
colour of the tie, the form of jewellery that was worn
on the day the page records. No detail is omitted and
a separate space is set aside for ' Remarks.' I remember
that I once asked Mr. Le V., half in jest, what he
should wear on the Judgment Day. Seriously, and (I
fancied) with a note of pathos in his voice, he said to
me, ' Young man, you ask me to lay bare my soul to
you. If I had been a saint I should certainly wear
a light suit, with a white waistcoat and a flower,
but I am no saint, sir, no saint. . . I shall probably
wear black trousers or trousers of some very dark
blue, and a frock-coat, tightly buttoned.' Poor old
Mr. Le V. ! I think he need not fear. If there be
a heaven for the soul, there must be other heavens
also, where the intellect and the body shall be consummate. In both these heavens Mr. Le V. will have
his hierarchy. Of a life like his there can be no conclusion, really. Did not even Matthew Arnold admit
that conduct of a cane is three-fourths of life ?

Certainly Mr. Le V. is a great artist, and his supremacy is in the tact with which he suits his toilet to
his temperament. But the marvellous affinity of a
dandy's mood to his daily toilet is not merely that it

27

finds therein its perfect echo nor that it may even be, in reflex, thereby accentuated or made less poignant. For some years I had felt convinced that in a perfect dandy this affinity must reach a point, when the costume itself, planned with the finest sensibility, would change with the emotional changes of its wearer, automatically. But I felt that here was one of those boundaries, where the fields of art align with the fields of science, and I hardly dared to venture further. Moreover, the theory was not easy to verify. I knew that, except in some great emotional crisis, the costume could not palpably change its aspect. Here was an *impasse;* for the perfect dandy—the Brummell, the Mr. Le V.—cannot afford to indulge in any great emotion outside his art ; like Balzac, he has not time. The gods were good to me, however. One morning near the end of last July, they decreed that I should pass through Half Moon Street and meet there a friend who should ask me to go with him to his club and watch for the results of the racing at Goodwood. This club includes hardly any member who is not a devotee of the Turf, so that, when we entered it, the cloak-room displayed long rows of unburdened pegs—save where one hat shone. None but that illustrious dandy,

28

Lord X., wears quite so broad a brim as this hat had. I said that Lord X. must be in the club.

'I conceive he is too nervous to be on the course,' my friend replied. 'They say he has plunged up to the hilt on to-day's running.'

His lordship was indeed there, fingering feverishly the sinuous ribands of the tape-machine. I sat at a little distance, watching him. Two results straggled forth within an hour, and, at the second of these, I saw with wonder Lord X.'s linen actually flush for a moment and then turn deadly pale. I looked again and saw that his boots had lost their lustre. Drawing nearer, I found that grey hairs had begun to show themselves in his raven coat. It was very painful and yet, to me, very gratifying. In the cloak-room, when I went for my own hat and cane, there was the hat with the broad brim, and (lo !) over its iron-blue surface little furrows had been ploughed by Despair.

Rouen, 1896.

A GOOD PRINCE

I first saw him one morning of last summer, in the Green Park. Though short, even insignificant, in stature and with an obvious tendency to be obese, he had that unruffled, Olympian air, which is so sure a sign of the Blood Royal. In a suit of white linen he looked serenely cool, despite the heat. Perhaps I should have thought him, had I not been versed in the *Almanach de Gotha*, a trifle older than he is. He did not raise his hat in answer to my salute, but smiled most graciously and made as though he would extend his hand to me, mistaking me, I doubt not, for one of his friends. Forthwith, a member of his suite said something to him in an undertone, whereat he smiled again and took no further notice of me.

I do not wonder the people idolise him. His almost blameless life has been passed among them, nothing in

33   c

it hidden from their knowledge. When they look upon his dear presentment in the photographer's window—the shrewd, kindly eyes under the high forehead, the sparse locks so carefully distributed—words of loyalty only and of admiration rise to their lips. For of all princes in modern days he seems to fulfil most perfectly the obligation of princely rank. Νήπιος he might have been called in the heroic age, when princes were judged according to their mastery of the sword or of the bow, or have seemed, to those mediæval eyes that loved to see a scholar's pate under the crown, an ignoramus. We are less exigent now. We do but ask of our princes that they should live among us, be often manifest to our eyes, set a perpetual example of a right life. We bid them be the ornaments of our State. Too often they do not attain to our ideal. They give, it may be, a half-hearted devotion to soldiering, or pursue pleasure merely—tales of their frivolity raising now and again the anger of a public swift to envy them their temptations. But against this admirable Prince no such charges can be made. Never (as yet, at least) has he cared to 'play at soldiers.' By no means has he shocked the Puritans. Though it is no secret that he prefers the society of ladies, not one

34

breath of scandal has ever tinged his name. Of how many English princes could this be said, in days when Figaro, quill in hand, inclines his ear to every key-hole ?

Upon the one action that were well obliterated from his record I need not long insist. It seems that the wife of an aged ex-Premier came to have an audience and pay her respects. Hardly had she spoken when the Prince, in a fit of unreasoning displeasure, struck her a violent blow with his clenched fist. Had His Royal Highness not always stood so far aloof from political contention, it had been easier to find a motive for this unmannerly blow. The incident is deplorable, but it belongs, after all, to an earlier period of his life ; and, were it not that no appreciation must rest upon the suppression of any scandal, I should not have referred to it. For the rest, I find no stain, soever faint, upon his life. The simplicity of his tastes is the more admirable for that he is known to care not at all for what may be reported in the newspapers. He has never touched a card, never entered a play-house. In no stud of racers has he indulged, preferring to the finest blood-horse ever bred a certain white and woolly lamb with a blue riband to its neck. This he is never

35

tired of fondling   It is with him, like the roebuck of
Henri Quatre, wherever he goes.

  Suave and simple his life is !   Narrow in range, it
may be, but with every royal appurtenance of delight,
for to him Love's happy favours are given and the
tribute of glad homage, always, here and there and
every other where.   Round the flower-garden at Sand-
ringham runs an old wall of red brick, streaked with
ivy and topped infrequently with balls of stone.   By
its iron gates, that open to a vista of flowers, stand two
kind policemen, guarding the Prince's procedure along
that bright vista.   As his perambulator rolls out of the
gate of St. James's Palace, he stretches out his tiny
hands to the scarlet sentinels.   An obsequious retinue
follows him over the lawns of the White Lodge, cooing
and laughing, blowing kisses and praising him.   Yet
do not imagine his life has been all gaiety !   The
afflictions that befall royal personages always touch very
poignantly the heart of the people, and it is not too
much to say that all England watched by the cradle-
side of Prince Edward in that dolorous hour, when
first the little battlements rose about the rose-red roof
of his mouth.   I am glad to think that not one
querulous word did His Royal Highness, in his great

agony, utter. They only say that his loud, incessant cries bore testimony to the perfect lungs for which the House of Hanover is most justly famed. Irreiterate be the horror of that epoch !

As yet, when we know not even what his first words will be, it is too early to predict what verdict posterity will pass upon him. Already he has won the hearts of the people ; but, in the years which, it is to be hoped, still await him, he may accomplish more. *Attendons !* He stands alone among European princes—but, as yet, only with the aid of a chair.

London, 1895.

1880

Say, shall these things be forgotten
In the Row that men call Rotten,
Beauty Clare ?—Hamilton Aïdé.

'History,' it has been said, 'does not repeat itself. The historians repeat one another.' Now, there are still some periods with which no historian has grappled, and, strangely enough, the period that most greatly fascinates me is one of them. The labour I set myself is therefore rather Herculean. But it is also, for me, so far a labour of love that I can quite forget or even revel in its great difficulty. I would love to have lived in those bygone days, when first society was inducted into the mysteries of art and, not losing yet its old and elegant *tenue*, babbled of blue china and white lilies, of the painter Rossetti and the poet Swinburne. It would be a splendid thing to have seen the *tableaux* at Cromwell

House or to have made my way through the Fancy Fair
and bartered all for a cigarette from a shepherdess ; to
have walked in the Park, straining my eyes for a
glimpse of the Jersey Lily ; danced the livelong afternoon to the strains of the Manola Valse ; clapped holes
in my gloves for Connie Gilchrist.

It is a pity that the historians have held back so long.
For this period is now so remote from us that much in
it is nearly impossible to understand, more than a little
must be left in the mists of antiquity that involve it.
The memoirs of the day are, indeed, many, but not
exactly illuminative.   From such writers as *Frith*, *Mon-
tague Williams* or the *Bancrofts*, you may gain but little

'Cromwell House.'   *The residence of Lady Freake, a famous hostess of
the day and founder of a brilliant* salon, *where even Royalty was sure of a
welcome.   The writer of a recent monograph declares that* 'many a
modern hostess would do well to emulate Lady Freake, not only in her
taste for the Beautiful in Art but also for the Intellectual in Conversation.'

'Fancy Fair.'   *For a full account of this function, see pp. 102–124 of
the* '*Annals of the Albert Hall.'*

'Jersey Lily.'   *A fanciful title bestowed, at this time, upon the beautiful Mrs. Langtry, who was a native of Jersey Island.   See also p. 51.*

'Manola Valse.'   *Supposed to have been introduced by Albert Edward,
Prince of Wales, who, having heard it in Vienna, was pleased, for a
while, by its novelty, but soon reverted to the more sprightly* deux-temps.

peculiar knowledge. That quaint old chronicler, *Lucy*, dilates amusingly enough upon the frown of Sir Richard (afterwards Lord) Cross or the tea-rose in the Prime Minister's button-hole. But what can he tell us of the negotiations that led Gladstone back to public life or of the secret councils of the Fourth Party, whereby Sir Stafford was gradually eclipsed ? Good memoirs must ever be the cumulation of gossip. Gossip (alas !) has been killed by the Press. In the tavern or the barber's-shop, all secrets passed into every ear. From newspapers how little can be culled ! Manifestations are there made manifest to us and we are taught, with tedious iteration, the things we knew, and need not have known, before. In my research, I have had only such poor guides as *Punch, or the London Charivari* and *The Queen, the Lady's Newspaper.* Excavation, which in the East has been productive of rich material for the archæologist, was indeed suggested to me. I was told that, just before Cleopatra's Needle was set upon the Embankment, an iron box, containing a photograph of Mrs. Langtry, some current coins and other trifles of the time, was dropped into the foundation. I am sure much might be done with a spade, here and there, in the neighbourhood of old Cromwell House. Accursed

43

be the obduracy of vestries ! Be not I, but they, blamed for any error, obscurity or omission in my brief excursus.

The period of 1880 and of the two successive years should ever be memorable, for it marks a great change in the constitution of English society. It would seem that, under the quiet *régime* of the Tory Cabinet, the upper ten thousand (as they were quaintly called in those days,) had taken a somewhat more frigid tone. The Prince of Wales had inclined to be restful after the revels of his youth. The prolonged seclusion of Queen Victoria, who was then engaged upon that superb work of introspection and self-analysis, *More Leaves from the Highlands*, had begun to tell upon the social system. Balls and other festivities, both at Court and in the houses of the nobles, were notably fewer. The vogue of the Opera was passing. Even in the top of the season, Rotten Row, I read, was not impenetrably crowded. But in 1880 came the tragic fall of Disraeli and the triumph of the Whigs. How great a change came then upon Westminster must be known to any one who has studied the annals of Gladstone's incomparable Parliament. Gladstone himself, with a monstrous majority behind him, revelling in the old splendour of speech that not seventy summers nor six years' sulking had made less ; Parnell, deadly, mysterious, with his crew of wordy peasants that were to set all Saxon things at naught—the activity of these two men alone would have made this Parliament supremely stimulating throughout the land. What of young Randolph Churchill, who, despite his halting speech, foppish mien and rather coarse fibre of mind, was yet the greatest Parliamentarian of his day ? What of Justin Huntly McCarthy, under his puerile mask a most dark, most dangerous conspirator, who, lightly swinging the sacred lamp of burlesque, irradiated with fearful clarity the wrath and sorrow of Ireland ? What of Blocker Warton ? What of the eloquent atheist, Charles Bradlaugh, pleading at the Bar, striding past the furious Tories to the very Mace, hustled down the stone steps with the broadcloth torn in ribands from his back ? Surely such scenes will never more be witnessed at St. Stephen's. Imagine the existence of God being made a party question ! No wonder that at a time of such turbulence fine society also should have shown the primordia of a great change. It was felt that the aristocracy could not live by good-breeding alone. The old delights seemed vapid, waxen. Some-

45

thing vivid was desired. And so the sphere of fashion converged with the sphere of art, and revolution was the result.

Be it remembered that long before this time there had been in the heart of Chelsea a kind of cult for Beauty. Certain artists had settled there, deliberately refusing to work in the ordinary official way, and ' wrought,' as they were wont to asseverate, ' for the pleasure and sake of all that is fair.' Little commerce had they with the brazen world. Nothing but the light of the sun would they share with men. Quietly and unbeknown, ʾcallous of all but their craft, they wrought their poems or their pictures, gave them one to another, and wrought on. Meredith, Rossetti, Swinburne, Morris, Holman Hunt were in this band of shy artificers. In fact, Beauty had existed long before 1880. It was Mr. Oscar Wilde who managed her *début*. To study the period is to admit that to him was due no small part of the social vogue that Beauty began to enjoy. Fired by his fervid words, men and women hurled their mahogany into the streets and ransacked the curio-shops for the furniture of Annish days. Dados arose upon every wall, sunflowers and

46

the feathers of peacocks curved in every corner, tea grew quite cold while the guests were praising the Willow Pattern of its cup. A few fashionable women even dressed themselves in sinuous draperies and unheard-of greens. Into whatsoever ballroom you went, you would surely find, among the women in tiaras and the fops and the distinguished foreigners, half a score of comely ragamuffins in velveteen, murmuring sonnets, posturing, waving their hands. Beauty was sought in the most unlikely places. Young painters found her mobled in the fogs, and bank-clerks, versed in the writings of Mr. Hamerton, were heard to declare, as they sped home from the City, that the Underground Railway was beautiful from London Bridge to Westminster, but not from Sloane Square to Notting Hill Gate.

Æstheticism (for so they named the movement,) did indeed permeate, in a manner, all classes. But it was to the *haut monde* that its primary appeal was made. The sacred emblems of Chelsea were sold in the fashionable toy-shops, its reverently chanted creeds became the patter of the *boudoirs*. The old Grosvenor Gallery, that stronghold of the few, was verily invaded.

47

Never was such a fusion of delightful folk as at its Private Views. There was Robert Browning, the philosopher, doffing his hat with a courtly sweep to more than one Duchess. There, too, was Theo Marzials, poet and eccentric, and Charles Colnaghi, the hero of a hundred tea-fights, and young Brookfield, the comedian, and many another good fellow. My Lord of Dudley, the *virtuoso*, came there, leaning for support upon the arm of his fair young wife. Disraeli, with his lustreless eyes and face like some seamed

'Private Views.' *This passage, which I found in a contemporary chronicle, is so quaint and so instinct with the spirit of its time that I am fain to quote it :*

'*There were quaint, beautiful, extraordinary costumes walking about— ultra-æsthetics, artistic-æsthetics, æsthetics that made up their minds to be daring, and suddenly gave way in some important point —put a frivolous bonnet on the top of a grave and flowing garment that Albert Durer might have designed for a mantle. There were fashionable costumes that Mrs. Mason or Madame Elise might have turned out that morning. The motley crowd mingled, forming into groups, sometimes dazzling you by the array of colours that you never thought to see in full daylight. . . . . Canary-coloured garments flitted cheerily by garments of the saddest green. A hat in an agony of pokes and angles was seen in company with a bonnet that was a gay garland of flowers. A vast cape that might have enshrouded the form of a Mater Dolorosa hung by the side of a jauntily-striped Langtry-hood.*'

Hebraic parchment, came also, and whispered behind his hand to the faithful Corry. And Walter Sickert spread the latest *mot* of 'the Master,' who, with monocle, cane and tilted hat, flashed through the gay mob anon.

Autrement, there was Coombe Wood, in whose shade the Lady Archibald Campbell suffered more than one of Shakespeare's plays to be enacted. Hither, from the garish, indelicate theatre that held her languishing, Thalia was bidden, if haply, under the open sky, she might resume her old charm. All Fashion came to marvel and so did all the Æsthetes, in the heart of one of whose leaders, Godwin, that superb architect, the idea was first conceived. Real Pastoral Plays ! Lest the invited guests should get any noxious scent of the footlights across the grass, only amateurs were accorded parts. They roved through a real wood, these jerkined amateurs, with the poet's music upon their lips. Never under such dark and griddled elms had the outlaws

---

The 'Master.' *By this title his disciples used to address James Whistler, the author-artist. Without echoing the obloquy that was lavished at first nor the praise that was lavished later upon his pictures, we must admit that he was, at least, a great master of English prose and a controversialist of no mean power.*

D

feasted upon their venison. Never had any Rosalind
traced with such shy wonder the writing of her lover
upon the bark, nor any Orlando won such laughter for
his not really sportive dalliance. Fairer than the
mummers, it may be, were the ladies who sat and
watched them from the lawn. All of them wore jerseys
and tied-back skirts. Zulu hats shaded their eyes from
the sun. Bangles shimmered upon their wrists. And
the gentlemen wore light frock-coats and light top-
hats with black bands. And the æsthetes were in
velveteen, carrying lilies.

Not that Art and Fashion shunned the theatre. They
began in 1880 to affect it as never before. The one
invaded Irving's *premières* at the Lyceum. The other
sang pæans in praise of the Bancrofts. The French
plays, too, were the feigned delight of all the modish
world. Not to have seen Chaumont in *Totot chez Tata*
was held a solecism. The homely mesdames and
messieurs from the Parisian boards were 'lionised'
(how strangely that phrase rings to modern ears !) in
ducal drawing-rooms. In fact, all the old prejudice
of rank was being swept away. Even more significant
than the reception of players was a certain effort, made
at this time, to raise the average of aristocratic loveli-

ness—an effort ' that, but a few years before, would
have been surely scouted as quite undignified and
outrageous. What the term 'Professional Beauty'
signified, how any lady gained a right to it, we do not
and may never know. It is certain, however, that
there were many ladies of tone, upon whom it was
bestowed. They received special attention from the
Prince of Wales, and hostesses would move heaven and
earth to have them in their rooms. Their photographs
were on sale in the window of every shop. Crowds
assembled every morning to see them start from Rotten
Row. Preëminent among Professional Beauties were
Lady Lonsdale (afterwards Lady de Grey), Mrs. Wheeler,
who always 'appeared in black,' and Mrs. Cornwallis
West, who was Amy Robsart in the *tableaux* at Cromwell
House, when Mrs. Langtry, *cette Cléopatre de son siècle*
appeared also, stepping across an artificial brook, in the
pink kirtle of Effie Deans. We may doubt whether the
movement, represented by these ladies, was quite in
accord with the dignity and elegance that always should
mark the best society. Any effort to make Beauty compulsory robs Beauty of its chief charm. But, at the same
time, I do believe that this movement, so far as it was
informed by a real wish to raise a practical standard of

feminine charm for all classes, does not deserve the
strictures that have been passed upon it by posterity.
One of its immediate sequels was the incursion of
American ladies into London. Then it was that these
pretty creatures, 'clad in Worth's most elegant con-
fections,' drawled their way through our greater portals.
Fanned, as they were, by the feathers of the Prince of
Wales, they had a great success, and they were so
strange that their voices and their dresses were
mimicked *partout*. The English beauties were rather
angry, especially with the Prince, whom alone they
blamed for the vogue of their rivals. History credits
His Royal Highness with many notable achievements.
Not the least of these is that he discovered the inhabitants of America.

It will be seen that in this renaissance the keenest
students of the exquisite were women. Nevertheless,
men were not idle, neither. Since the day of Mr.
Brummell and King George, the noble art of self-
adornment had fallen partially desuete. Great fops
like Bulwer and *le jeune Cupidon* had come upon the
town, but never had they formed a school. Dress,
therefore, had become simpler, wardrobes smaller,
fashions apt to linger. In 1880 arose the sect that

was soon to win for itself the title of 'The Mashers.'
What this title exactly signified I suppose no two
etymologists will ever agree. But we can learn clearly
enough, from the fashion-plates of the day, what the
Mashers were in outward semblance ; from the lampoons, their mode of life. Unlike the dandies of the
Georgian era, they pretended to no classic taste and,
wholly contemptuous of the Æsthetes, recognised no
art save the art of dress. Much might be written
about the Mashers. The restaurant—destined to be,
in after years, so salient a delight of London—was not
known to them, but they were often admirable upon
the steps of clubs. The Lyceum held them never,
but nightly they gathered at the Gaiety Theatre.
Nightly the stalls were agog with small, sleek heads
surmounting collars of interminable height. Nightly,
in the *foyer*, were lisped the praises of Kate Vaughan,
her graceful dancing, or of Nellie Farren, her match-

'Masher.'   *One authority derives the title, rather ingeniously, from*
'*Ma Chère,*' *the mode of address used by the gilded youth to the bar-
maids of the period—whence the corruption* '*Masher.*'   *Another traces
it to the chorus of a song, which, at that time, had a great vogue in the
music-halls :*

'*I'm the slashing, dashing, mashing Montmorency of the day.*'
This, in my opinion, is the safer suggestion, and may be adopted.

53

less fooling. Never a night passed but the dreary
stage-door was cinct with a circlet of fools bearing
bright bouquets, of flaxen-headed fools who had feet
like black needles, and graceful fools incumbent upon
canes. A strange cult! I once knew a lady whose
father was actually present at the first night of 'The
Forty Thieves,' and fell enamoured of one of the *cory-
phées*. By such links is one age joined to another.

There is always something rather absurd about the
past. For us, who have fared on, the silhouette of Error
is sharp upon the past horizon. As we look back upon
any period, its fashions seem grotesque, its ideals
shallow, for we know how soon those ideals and those
fashions were to perish, and how rightly; nor can we
feel a little of the fervour they did inspire. It is easy
to laugh at these Mashers, with their fantastic raiment
and languid lives, or at the strife of the Professional
Beauties. It is easy to laugh at all that ensued when
first the mummers and the stainers of canvas strayed
into Mayfair. Yet shall I laugh? For me the most
romantic moment of a pantomime is always when the
winged and wired fairies begin to fade away, and, as
they fade, clown and pantaloon tumble on joppling
and grimacing, seen very faintly in that indecisive twi-

54

light.   The social condition of 1880 fascinates me in the same way.   Its contrasts fascinate me.

Perhaps, in my study of the period, I may have fallen so deeply beneath its spell that I have tended, now and again, to overrate its real import.   I lay no claim to the true historical spirit.   I fancy it was a chalk drawing of a girl in a mob-cap, signed ' Frank Miles, 1880,' that first impelled me to research.   To give an accurate and exhaustive account of that period would need a far less brilliant pen than mine.   But I hope that, by dealing, even so briefly as I have dealt, with its more strictly sentimental aspects, I may have lightened the task of the scientific historian.   And I look to Professor Gardiner and to the Bishop of Oxford.

London, 1894.

KING GEORGE THE FOURTH

They say that when King George was dying, a special form of prayer for his recovery, composed by one of the Archbishops, was read aloud to him and that His Majesty, after saying Amen 'thrice, with great fervour,' begged that his thanks might be conveyed to its author. To the student of royalty in modern times there is something rather suggestive in this incident. I like to think of the drug-scented room at Windsor and of the King, livid and immobile among his pillows, waiting, in superstitious awe, for the near moment when he must stand, a spirit, in the presence of a perpetual King. I like to think of him following the futile prayer with eyes and lips, and then, custom resurgent in him and a touch of pride that, so long as the blood moved ever so little in his veins, he was still a king, expressing a desire that the dutiful feeling and

59

admirable taste of the Prelate should receive a suitable acknowledgment. It would have been impossible for a real monarch like George, even after the gout had turned his thoughts heavenward, really to abase himself before his Maker. But he could, so to say, treat with Him, as he might have treated with a fellow-sovereign, in a formal way, long after diplomacy was quite useless. How strange it must be to be a king! How delicate and difficult a task it is to judge him! So far as I know, no attempt has been made to judge King George the Fourth fairly. The hundred and one eulogies and lampoons, irresponsibly published during and immediately after his reign, are not worth a wooden hoop in Hades. Mr. Percy Fitzgerald has published a history of George's reign, in which he has so artistically subordinated his own personality to his subject, that I can scarcely find, from beginning to end of the two bulky volumes, a single opinion expressed, a single idea, a single deduction from the admirably-ordered facts. All that most of us know of George is from Thackeray's brilliant denunciation. Now, I yield to few in my admiration of Thackeray's powers. He had a charming style. We never find him searching for the *mot juste* as for a needle in a bottle of hay. Could he have

60

looked through a certain window by the river at Croisset or in the quadrangle at Brasenose, how he would have laughed! He blew on his pipe, and words came tripping round him, like children, like pretty little children who are perfectly drilled for the dance, or came, did he will it, treading in their precedence, like kings, gloomily. And I think it is to the credit of the reading mob that, by reason of his beautiful style, all that he said was taken for the truth, without questioning. But truth after all is eternal, and style transient, and now that Thackeray's style is becoming, if I may say so, a trifle 1860, it may not be amiss that we should inquire whether his estimate of George is in substance and fact worth anything at all. It seems to me that, as in his novels, so in his history of the four Georges, Thackeray made no attempt at psychology. He dealt simply with types. One George he insisted upon regarding as a buffoon, another as a yokel. The Fourth George he chose to hold up for reprobation as a drunken, vapid cad. Every action, every phase of his life that went to disprove this view, he either suppressed or distorted utterly. 'History,' he would seem to have chuckled, 'has nothing to do with the First Gentleman. But I will give him a niche in Natural

History. He shall be King of the Beasts.' He made no allowance for the extraordinary conditions under which all monarchs live, none for the unfortunate circumstances by which George, especially, was from the first hampered. He judged him as he judged Barnes Newcome and all the scoundrels he created. Moreover, he judged him by the moral standard of the Victorian Age. In fact, he applied to his subject the wrong method, in the wrong manner, and at the wrong time. And yet every one has taken him at his word. I feel that my essay may be scouted as a paradox ; but I hope that many may recognise that I am not, out of mere boredom, endeavouring to stop my ears against popular platitude, but rather, in a spirit of real earnestness, to point out to the mob how it has been cruel to George. I do not despair of success. I think I shall make converts. The mob is really very fickle and sometimes cheers the truth.

None, at all events, will deny that England stands to-day otherwise than she stood a hundred and thirty-two years ago, when George was born. To-day we are living a decadent life. All the while that we are prating of progress, we are really so deteriorate ! There is nothing but feebleness in us. Our youths, who spend their days in trying to build up their constitutions by sport or athletics and their evenings in undermining them with poisonous and dyed drinks ; our daughters, who are ever searching for some new quack remedy for new imaginary megrim, what strength is there in them ? We have our societies for the prevention of this and the promotion of that and the propagation of the other, because there are no individuals among us. Our sexes are already nearly assimilate. Women are becoming nearly as rare as ladies, and it is only at the music-halls that we are privileged to see strong men. We are born into a poor, weak age. We are not strong enough to be wicked, and the Nonconformist Conscience makes cowards of us all.

But this was not so in the days when George was walking by his tutor's side in the gardens of Kew or of Windsor. London must have been a splendid place in those days—full of life and colour and wrong and revelry. There was no absurd press nor vestry to protect the poor at the expense of the rich and see that everything should be neatly adjusted. Every man had to shift for himself and, consequently, men were, as Mr. Clement Scott would say, manly, and women, as Mr. Clement Scott would say, womanly. In those days, a young man of wealth and family found open to him a vista of such licence as had been unknown to any since the barbatuli of the Roman Empire. To spend the early morning with his valet, gradually assuming the rich apparel that was not then tabooed by a hard sumptuary standard; to saunter round to White's for ale and tittle-tattle and the making of wagers; to attend a ' drunken *déjeuner* ' in honour of ' *la très belle Rosaline* ' or the Strappini; to drive some fellow-fool far out into the country in his pretty curricle, ' followed by two well-dressed and well-mounted grooms, of singular elegance certainly,' and stop at every tavern on the road to curse the host for not keeping better ale and a wench of more charm; to reach St. James's in time for a random toilet and so off to dinner. Which of *our* dandies could survive a day of pleasure such as this? Which would be ready, dinner done, to scamper off again to Ranelagh and dance and skip and sup in the rotunda there? Yet the youth of that period would not dream of going to bed or ever he had looked in at Crockford's—*tanta lubido rerum*—for a few hours' faro.

This was the kind of life that young George found opened to him, when, at length, in his nineteenth year, they gave him an establishment in Buckingham House. How his young eyes must have sparkled, and with what glad gasps must he have taken the air of freedom into his lungs ! Rumour had long been busy with the damned surveillance under which his childhood had been passed. A paper of the time says significantly that ' the Prince of Wales, with a spirit which does him honour, has three times requested a change in that system.' King George had long postponed permission for his son to appear at any balls, and the year before had only given it, lest he should offend the Spanish Minister, who begged it as a personal favour. I know few pictures more pathetic than that of George, then an overgrown boy of fourteen, tearing the childish frill from around his neck and crying to one of the Royal servants, ' See how they treat me ! ' Childhood has always seemed to me the tragic period of life. To be subject to the most odious espionage at the one age when you never dream of doing wrong, to be deceived by your parents, thwarted of your smallest wish, oppressed by the terrors of manhood and of the world to come, and to believe, as you are told, that childhood is the only happiness known ; all this is quite terrible. And all Royal children, of whom I have read, parti-

E

cularly George, seem to have passed through greater trials in childhood than do the children of any other class. Mr. Fitzgerald, hazarding for once an opinion, thinks that 'the stupid, odious, German, sergeant-system of discipline that had been so rigorously applied was, in fact, responsible for the blemishes of the young Prince's character.' Even Thackeray, in his essay upon George III., asks what wonder that the son, finding himself free at last, should have plunged, without looking, into the vortex of dissipation. In Torrens' *Life of Lord Melbourne* we learn that Lord Essex, riding one day with the King, met the young Prince wearing a wig, and that the culprit, being sternly reprimanded by his father, replied that he had 'been ordered by his doctor to wear a wig, for he was subject to cold.' Whereupon the King, to vent the aversion he already felt for his son, or, it may have been, glorying in the satisfactory result of his discipline, turned to Lord Essex and remarked, 'A lie is ever ready when it is wanted.' George never lost this early-ingrained habit of lies. It is to George's childish fear of his guardians that we must trace that extra-ordinary power of bamboozling his courtiers, his ministry, and his mistresses that distinguished him through his

66

long life. It is characteristic of the man that he should himself have bitterly deplored his own untruthfulness. When, in after years, he was consulting Lady Spencer upon the choice of a governess for his child, he made this remarkable speech, 'Above all, she must be taught the truth. You know that I don't speak the truth and my brothers don't, and I find it a great defect, from which I would have my daughter free. *We have been brought up badly, the Queen having taught us to equivocate.'* . You may laugh at the picture of the little chubby, curly-headed fellows learning to equivocate at their mother's knee, but pray remember that the wisest master of ethics himself, in his theory of ἕξεις ἀποδείκτικαι, similarly raised virtues, such as telling the truth, to the level of regular accomplishments, and, before you judge poor George harshly in his entanglements of lying, think of the cruelly unwise education he had undergone.

However much we may deplore this exaggerated tyranny, by reason of its evil effect upon his moral nature, we cannot but feel glad that it existed, to afford a piquant contrast to the life awaiting him. Had he passed through the callow dissipations of Eton and Oxford, like other young men of his age, he would

assuredly have lacked much of that splendid, pent
vigour with which he rushed headlong into London
life.   He was   so   young and so   handsome and
so strong, that can we wonder if all the women
fell at his feet ?   ' The graces of his person,' says one
whom he honoured by an intrigue, ' the irresistible
sweetness of his smile, the tenderness of his melodious,
yet manly voice, will be remembered by me till every
vision of this changing scene are forgotten.   The
polished and fascinating ingenuousness of his manners
contributed not a little to enliven our promenade.
He sang with exquisite taste, and the tones of his voice,
breaking on the silence of the night, have often
appeared to my entranced senses like more than mortal
melody.'   But besides his graces of person, he had a
most delightful wit, he was a scholar who could bandy
quotations with Fox or Sheridan, and, like the young
men of to-day, he knew all about Art.   He spoke
French, Italian, and German perfectly.   Crossdill had
taught him the violoncello.   At first, as was right for
one of his age, he cared more for the pleasures of the
table and of the ring, for cards and love.   He was
wont to go down to Ranelagh surrounded by a retinue
of bruisers—rapscallions, such as used to follow Clodius

through the streets of Rome—and he loved to join
in the scuffles like any commoner. Pugilism he learnt
from Angelo, and he was considered by some to be a
fine performer. On one occasion, too, at an *exposition
d'escrime*, when he handled the foils against the *maître*,
he 'was highly complimented upon his graceful
postures.' In fact, despite all his accomplishments, he
seems to have been a thoroughly manly young fellow.
He was just the kind of figure-head Society had long
been in need of. A certain lack of tone had crept
into the amusements of the *haut monde*, due, doubtless,
to the lack of an acknowledged leader. The King
was not yet mad, but he was always bucolic, and
socially out of the question. So at the coming of his
son Society broke into a gallop. Balls and masquerades
were given in his honour night after night. Good
Samaritans must have approved when they found that
at these entertainments great ladies and courtesans
brushed beautiful shoulders in utmost familiarity, but
those who delighted in the high charm of society
probably shook their heads. We need not, however,
find it a flaw in George's social bearing that he did not
check this kind of freedom. At the first, as a young
man full of life, of course he took everything as it

came, joyfully. No one knew better than he did, in later life, that there is a time for laughing with great ladies and a time for laughing with courtesans. But as yet it was not possible for him to exert influence. How great that influence became I will suggest hereafter.

I like to think of him as he was at this period, charging about, in pursuit of pleasure, like a young bull. The splendid taste for building had not yet come to him. His father would not hear of him patronising the Turf. But already he was implected with a passion for dress and seems to have erred somewhat on the side of dressing up, as is the way of young men. It is fearful to think of him, as Cyrus Redding saw him, 'arrayed in deep-brown velvet, silver embroidered, with cut-steel buttons, and a gold net thrown over all.' Before that 'gold net thrown over all,' all the mistakes of his after-life seem to me to grow almost insignificant. Time, however, toned his too florid sense of costume, and we should at any rate be thankful that his imagination never deserted him. All the delightful munditiæ that we find in the contemporary 'fashion-plates for gentle-men' can be traced to George himself. His were the much-approved 'quadruple stock of great dimension,'

the ' cocked grey-beaver,' ' the pantaloons of mauve silk
negligently crinkled' and any number of other little
pomps and foibles of the kind. As he grew older and
was obliged to abandon many of his more vigorous
pastimes, he grew more and more enamoured of
the pleasures of the wardrobe. He would spend
hours, it is said, in designing coats for his friends,
liveries for his servants, and even uniforms. Nor did
he ever make the mistake of giving away outmoded
clothes to his valets, but kept them to form what must
have been the finest collection of clothes that has been
seen in modern times. With a sentimentality that is
characteristic of him, he would often, as he sat, crippled
by gout, in his room at Windsor, direct his servant to
bring him this or that coat, which he had worn ten or
twenty or thirty years before, and, when it was brought
to him, spend much time in laughing or sobbing over
the memories that lay in its folds. It is pleasant to
know that George, during his long and various life,
never forgot a coat, however long ago worn, however
seldom.

But in the early days of which I speak he had not
yet touched that self-conscious note which, in manner
and mode of life, as well as in costume, he was to

touch later. He was too violently enamoured of all around him, to think very deeply of himself. But he had already realised the tragedy of the voluptuary, which is, after a little time, not that he must go on living, but that he cannot live in two places at once. We have, at this end of the century, tempered this tragedy by the perfection of railways, and it is possible for our good Prince, whom Heaven bless, to waken to the sound of the Braemar bagpipes, while the music of Mdlle. Guilbert's latest song, cooed over the footlights of the Concerts Parisiens, still rings in his ears. But in the time of our Prince's illustrious great-uncle there were not railways ; and we find George perpetually driving, for wagers, to Brighton and back (he had already acquired that taste for Brighton which was one of his most loveable qualities) in incredibly short periods of time. The rustics who lived along the road were well accustomed to the sight of a high, tremulous phaeton flashing past them, and the crimson face of the young Prince bending over the horses. There is something absurd in representing George as, even before he came of age, a hardened and cynical profligate, an Elagabalus in trousers. His blood flowed fast enough through his veins. All his escapades were

those of a healthful young man of the time. Need
we blame him if he sought, every day, to live faster
and more fully ?

In a brief essay like this, I cannot attempt to write,
as I hope one day to do, in any detail a history of
George's career, during the time when he was succes-
sively Prince of Wales and Regent and King. Merely
is it my wish at present to examine some of the prin-
cipal accusations that have been brought against him,
and to point out in what ways he has been harshly
and hastily judged. Perhaps the greatest indignation
against him was, and is to this day, felt by reason of
his treatment of his two wives, Mrs. Fitzherbert and
Queen Caroline. There are some scandals that never
grow old, and I think the story of George's married
life is one of them. It was a real scandal. I can feel
it. It has vitality. Often have I wondered whether
the blood with which the young Prince's shirt was
saturate when Mrs. Fitzherbert was first induced to
visit him at Carlton House, was merely red paint, or if,
in a frenzy of love, he had truly gashed himself with
a razor. Certain it is that his passion for the virtuous
and obdurate lady was a very real one. Lord Holland
describes how the Prince used to visit Mrs. Fox, and

73

there indulge in ' the most extravagant expressions and
actions—rolling on the floor, striking his forehead,
tearing his hair, falling into hysterics, and swearing
that he would abandon the country, forego the crown,
&c.' He was indeed still a child, for Royalties, not
being ever brought into contact with the realities of
life, remain young far longer than other people.
Cursed with a truly royal lack of self-control, he was
unable to bear the idea of being thwarted in any wish.
Every day he sent off couriers to Holland, whither
Mrs. Fitzherbert had retreated, imploring her to return
to him, offering her formal marriage. At length, as
we know, she yielded to his importunity and returned.
It is difficult indeed to realise exactly what was Mrs.
Fitzherbert's feeling in the matter. The marriage
must be, as she knew, illegal, and would lead, as
Charles James Fox pointed out in his powerful letter
to the Prince, to endless and intricate difficulties. For
the present she could only live with him as his mistress.
If, when he reached the legal age of twenty-five, he
were to apply to Parliament for permission to marry
her, how could permission be given, when she had been
living with him irregularly ? Doubtless, she was flattered by the attentions of the Heir to the Throne, but,

74

had she really returned his passion, she would surely have preferred 'any other species of connection with His Royal Highness to one leading to so much misery and mischief.' Really to understand her marriage, one must look at the portraits of her that are extant. That beautiful and silly face explains much. One can well fancy such a lady being pleased to live after the performance of a mock-ceremony with a prince for whom she felt no passion. Her view of the matter can only have been social, for, in the eyes of the Church, she could only live with the Prince as his mistress. Society, however, once satisfied that a ceremony of some kind had been enacted, never regarded her as anything but his wife. The day after Fox, inspired by the Prince, had formally denied that any ceremony had taken place, 'the knocker of her door,' to quote her own complacent phrase, 'was never still.' The Duchesses of Portland, Devonshire and Cumberland were among her visitors.

How much pop-limbo has been talked about the Prince's denial of the marriage! I grant that it was highly improper to marry Mrs. Fitzherbert at all. But George was always weak and wayward, and he did, in his great passion, marry her. That he should after-

75

wards deny it officially seems to me to have been utterly inevitable. His denial did her not the faintest damage, as I have pointed out. It was, so to speak, an official quibble, rendered necessary by the circumstances of the case. Not to have denied the marriage in the House of Commons would have meant ruin to both of them. As months passed, more serious difficulties awaited the unhappily wedded pair. What boots it to repeat the story of the Prince's great debts and desperation ? It was clear that there was but one way of getting his head above water, and that was to yield to his father's wishes and contract a real marriage with a foreign princess. Fate was dogging his footsteps relentlessly. Placed as he was, George could not but offer to marry as his father willed. It is well, also, to remember that George was not ruthlessly and suddenly turning his shoulder upon Mrs. Fitzherbert. For some time before the British plenipotentiary went to fetch him a bride from over the waters, his name had been associated with that of the beautiful and unscrupulous Countess of Jersey.

Poor George ! Half-married to a woman whom he no longer worshipped, compelled to marry a woman whom he was to hate at first sight ! Surely we should not judge a prince harshly. 'Princess Caroline very *gauche* at cards,' 'Princess Caroline very *missish* at supper,' are among the entries made in his diary by Lord Malmesbury, while he was at the little German Court. I can conceive no scene more tragic than that of her presentation to the Prince, as related by the same nobleman. ' I, according to the established etiquette,' so he writes, 'introduced the Princess Caroline to him. She, very properly, in consequence of my saying it was the right mode of proceeding, attempted to kneel to him. He raised her gracefully enough, and embraced her, said barely one word, turned round, retired to a distant part of the apartment, and calling to me, said : ' Harris, I am not well : pray get me a glass of brandy.' At dinner that evening, in the presence of her betrothed, the Princess was ' flippant, rattling, affecting wit.' Poor George, I say again ! Deportment was his ruling passion, and his bride did not know how to behave. Vulgarity—hard, implacable, German vulgarity—was in everything she did to the very day of her death. The marriage was solemnised on Wednesday, April 8th, 1795, and the royal bridegroom was drunk.

So soon as they were separated, George became

77

implected with a morbid hatred for his wife, which was hardly in accord with his light and variant nature and shows how bitterly he had been mortified by his marriage of necessity. It is sad that so much of his life should have been wasted in futile strainings after divorce. Yet we can scarcely blame him for seizing upon every scrap of scandal that was whispered of his wife. Besides his not unnatural wish to be free, it was derogatory to the dignity of a prince and a regent that his wife should be living an eccentric life at Blackheath with a family of singers named Sapio. Indeed, Caroline's conduct during this time was as indiscreet as ever. Wherever she went she made ribald jokes about her husband, ' in such a voice that all, by-standing, might hear.' ' After dinner,' writes one of her servants, ' Her Royal Highness made a wax figure as usual, and gave it an amiable pair of large horns ; then took three pins out of her garment and stuck them through and through, and put the figure to roast and melt at the fire. What a silly piece of spite ! Yet it is impossible not to laugh when one sees it done.' Imagine the feelings of the First Gentleman in Europe when the unseemly story of these pranks was whispered to him !

78

For my own part, I fancy Caroline was innocent of any infidelity to her unhappy husband. But that is neither here nor there. Her behaviour was certainly not above suspicion. It fully justified George in trying to establish a case for her divorce. When, at length, she went abroad, her vagaries were such that the whole of her English suite left her, and we hear of her travelling about the Holy Land attended by another family, named Bergami. When her husband succeeded to the throne, and her name was struck out of the liturgy, she despatched expostulations in absurd English to Lord Liverpool. Receiving no answer, she decided to return and claim her right to be crowned Queen of England. Whatever the unhappy lady did, she always was ridiculous. One cannot but smile as one reads of her posting along the French roads in a yellow travelling-chariot drawn by cart-horses, with a retinue that included an alderman, a reclaimed lady-in-waiting, an Italian count, the eldest son of the alderman, and 'a fine little female child, about three years old, whom Her Majesty, in conformity with her benevolent practices on former occasions, had adopted.' The breakdown of her impeachment, and her acceptance of an income formed a fitting anti-climax to the terrible absurdities of her position. She died from the effects of a chill caught when she was trying vainly to force a way to her husband's coronation. Unhappy woman ! Our sympathy for her is not misgiven. Fate wrote her a most tremendous tragedy, and she played it in tights. Let us pity her, but not forget to pity her husband, the King, also.

It is another common accusation against George that he was an undutiful and unfeeling son. If this was so, it is certain that not all the blame is to be laid upon him alone. There is more than one anecdote which shows that King George disliked his eldest son, and took no trouble to conceal his dislike, long before the boy had been freed from his tutors. It was the coldness of his father and the petty restrictions he loved to enforce that first drove George to seek the companionship of such men as Egalité and the Duke of Cumberland, both of whom were quick to inflame his impressionable mind to angry resentment. Yet, when Margaret Nicholson attempted the life of the King, the Prince immediately posted off from Brighton that he might wait upon his father at Windsor—a graceful act of piety that was rewarded by his father's refusal to see him. Hated by the Queen, who at this time did all she could to keep her husband and his son apart, surrounded by intriguers, who did all they could to set him against his father, George seems to have behaved with great discretion. In the years that follow, I can conceive no position more difficult than that in which he found himself every time his father relapsed into lunacy. That he should have by every means opposed those who through jealousy stood between him and the regency was only natural. It cannot be said that at any time did he show anxiety to rule, so long as there was any immediate chance of the King's recovery. On the contrary, all impartial seers of that chaotic Court agreed that the Prince bore himself throughout the intrigues, wherein he himself was bound to be, in a notably filial way.

There are many things that I regret in the career of George IV., and what I most of all regret is the part that he played in the politics of the period. Englishmen to-day have at length decided that Royalty shall not set foot in the political arena. I do not despair that some day we shall place politics upon a sound commercial basis, as they have already done in America and France, or leave them entirely in the hands of the police, as they do in Russia. It is horrible to think

that, under our existing *régime*, all the men of noblest
blood and highest intellect should waste their time in
the sordid atmosphere of the House of Commons,
listening for hours to nonentities talking nonsense, or
searching enormous volumes to prove that somebody
said something some years ago that does not quite tally
with something he said the other day, or standing
tremulous before the whips in the lobbies and the
scorpions in the constituencies. In the political
machine are crushed and lost all our best men. That
Mr. Gladstone did not choose to be a cardinal is a blow
under which the Roman Catholic Church still staggers.
In Mr. Chamberlain Scotland Yard missed its smartest
detective. What a fine voluptuary might Lord Rosebery
have been ! It is a platitude that the country is ruled
best by the permanent officials, and I look forward to
the time when Mr. Keir Hardie shall hang his cap in
the hall of No. 10 Downing Street, and a Conservative
working man shall lead Her Majesty's Opposition. In
the lifetime of George, politics were not a whit finer
than they are to-day. I feel a genuine indignation that
he should have wasted so much of tissue in mean
intrigues about ministries and bills. That he should
have been fascinated by that splendid fellow, Fox, is

82

quite right. That he should have thrown himself with all his heart into the storm of the Westminster election is most natural. But it is awful inverideed to find him, long after he had reached man's estate, indulging in back-stair intrigues with Whigs and Tories. It is, of course, absurd to charge him with deserting his first friends, the Whigs. His love and fidelity were given, not to the Whigs, but to the men who led them. Even after the death of Fox, he did, in misplaced piety, do all he could for Fox's party. What wonder that, when he found he was ignored by the Ministry that owed its existence to him, he turned his back upon that sombre couple, the ' Lords G. and G.,' whom he had always hated, and went over to the Tories ? Among the Tories he hoped to find men who would faithfully perform their duties and leave him leisure to live his own beautiful life. I regret immensely that his part in politics did not cease here. The state of the country and of his own finances, and also, I fear, a certain love that he had imbibed for political manipulation, prevented him from standing aside. How useless was all the finesse he displayed in the long-drawn question of Catholic Emancipation ! How lamentable his terror of Lord Wellesley's rude dragooning ! And is there not something pitiable in the thought of the Regent at a time of ministerial complications lying prone on his bed with a sprained ankle, and taking, as was whispered, in one day as many as seven hundred drops of laudanum ? Some said he took these doses to deaden the pain. But others, and among them his brother Cumberland, declared that the sprain was all a sham. I hope it was. The thought of a voluptuary in pain is very terrible. In any case, I cannot but feel angry, for George's own sake and that of his kingdom, that he found it impossible to keep further aloof from the wearisome troubles of political life. His wretched indecision of character made him an easy prey to unscrupulous ministers, while his extraordinary diplomatic powers and almost extravagant tact made them, in their turn, an easy prey to him. In these two processes much of his genius was spent untimely. I must confess that he did not quite realise where his duties ended. He wished always to do too much. If you read his repeated appeals to his father that he might be permitted to serve actively in the British army against the French, you will acknowledge that it was through no fault of his own that he did not fight. It touches me to think that in his declining years he

84

actually thought that he had led one of the charges at Waterloo. He would often describe the whole scene as it appeared to him at that supreme moment, and refer to the Duke of Wellington, saying, 'Was it not so, Duke?' 'I have often heard you say so, your Majesty,' the old soldier would reply, grimly. I am not sure that the old soldier was at Waterloo himself. In a room full of people he once referred to the battle as having been won upon the playing-fields of Eton. This was certainly a most unfortunate slip, seeing that all historians are agreed that it was fought on a certain field situate a few miles from Brussels.

In one of his letters to the King, craving for a military appointment, George urges that, whilst his next brother, the Duke of York, commanded the army, and the younger branches of the family were either generals or lieutenant-generals, he, who was Prince of Wales, remained colonel of dragoons. And herein, could he have known it, lay the right limitation of his life. As Royalty was and is constituted, it is for the younger sons to take an active part in the services, whilst the eldest son is left as the ruler of Society. Thousands and thousands of guineas were given by the nation that the Prince of Wales, the Regent, the King, might be, in the best sense of the word, ornamental. It is not for us, at this moment, to consider whether Royalty, as a wholly Pagan institution, is not out of place in a community of Christians. It is enough that we should inquire whether the god, whom our grandfathers set up and worshipped and crowned with offerings, gave grace to his worshippers.

That George was a moral man, in our modern sense, I do not for one moment pretend. It were idle to deny that he was profligate. When he died there were found in one of his cabinets more than a hundred locks of women's hair. Some of these were still plastered with powder and pomatum, some were mere little golden curls, such as grow low down upon a girl's neck, others were streaked with grey. The whole of this collection subsequently passed into the hands of Adam, the famous Scotch henchman of the Regent. In his family, now resident in Glasgow, it is treasured as an heirloom. I myself have been privileged to look at all these locks of hair, and I have seen a *clairvoyante* take them one by one, and, pinching them between her lithe fingers, tell of the love that each symbolised. I have heard her tell of long rides by night, of a boudoir hung with grass-green satin, and of a tryst at Windsor ; of one, the wife of a hussar at York, whose little lap-dog used to bark angrily whenever the Regent came near his mistress ; of a milkmaid who, in her great simpleness, thought her child would one day be King of England ; of an arch-duchess with blue eyes, and a silly little flautist from Portugal ; of women that were wantons and fought for his favour, great ladies that he loved dearly, girls that gave themselves to him humbly. If we lay all pleasures at the feet of our Prince, we can scarcely hope he will remain virtuous. Indeed, we do not wish our Prince to be an examplar of godliness, but a perfect type of happiness. It may be foolish of us to insist upon apolaustic happiness, but that is the kind of happiness that we can ourselves, most of us, best understand, and so we offer it to our ideal. In Royalty we find our Bacchus, our Venus.

Certainly George was, in the practical sense of the word, a fine king. His wonderful physique, his wealth, his brilliant talents, he gave them all without stint to Society. From the time when, at Madame Cornelys', he gallivanted with rips and demireps, to the time when he sat, a stout and solitary old king, fishing in the artificial pond at Windsor, his life was beautifully

87

ordered. He indulged to the full in all the delights
that England could offer him. That he should have,
in his old age, suddenly abandoned his career of
vigorous enjoyment is, I confess, rather surprising.
The Royal voluptuary generally remains young to the
last. No one ever tires of pleasure. It is the pursuit
of pleasure, the trouble to grasp it, that makes us old.
Only the soldiers who enter Capua with wounded feet
leave it demoralised. And yet George, who never had
to wait or fight for a pleasure, fell enervate long before
his death. I can but attribute this to the constant persecution to which he was subjected by duns and
ministers, parents and wives.

Not that I regret the manner in which he spent his
last years. On the contrary, I think it was exceed-
ingly cosy. I like to think of the King, at Windsor,
lying a-bed all the morning in his darkened room, with
all the sporting papers scattered over his quilt and a
little decanter of the favourite cherry-brandy within
easy reach. I like to think of him sitting by his fire
in the afternoon and hearing his ministers ask for him
at the door and piling another log upon the fire, as he
heard them sent away by his servant. It was not, I
acknowledge, a life to kindle popular enthusiasm.

But most people knew little of its mode. For all they knew, His Majesty might have been making his soul or writing his memoirs. In reality, George was now ' too fat by far ' to brook the observation of casual eyes. Especially he hated to be seen by those whose memories might bear them back to the time when he had yet a waist. Among his elaborate precautions of privacy was a pair of *avant-couriers*, who always preceded his pony-chaise in its daily progress through Windsor Great Park and had strict commands to drive back any intruder. In *The Veiled Majestic Man, Where is the Graceful Despot of England?* and other lampoons not extant, the scribblers mocked his loneliness. At White's, one evening, four gentlemen of high fashion vowed, over their wine, they would see the invisible monarch. So they rode down next day to Windsor, and secreted themselves in the branches of a holm-oak. Here they waited *perdus*, beguiling the hours and the frost with their flasks. When dusk was falling, they heard at last the chime of hoofs on the hard road, and saw presently a splash of the Royal livery, as two grooms trotted by, peering warily from side to side, and disappeared in the gloom. The conspirators in the tree held their breath, till they caught the distant sound

89

of wheels. Nearer and louder came the sound, and soon they saw a white, postillioned pony, a chaise and, yes, girth immensurate among the cushions, a weary monarch, whose face, crimson above the dark accumulation of his stock, was like some ominous sunset. . . . He had passed them and they had seen him, monstrous and moribund among the cushions. He had been borne past them like a wounded Bacchanal. The King! The Regent! . . . They shuddered in the frosty branches. The night was gathering and they climbed silently to the ground, with an awful, indispellible image before their eyes.

You see, these gentlemen were not philosophers. Remember, also, that the strangeness of their escapade, the cramped attitude they had been compelled to maintain in the branches of the holm-oak, the intense cold and their frequent resort to the flask must have all conspired to exaggerate their emotions and prevent them from looking at things in a rational way. After all, George had lived his life. He had lived more fully than any other man. And it was better really that his death should be preceded by decline. For every one, obviously, the most *desirable* kind of death is that which strikes men down, suddenly, in their prime. Had they not been so dangerous, railways would never have ousted the old coaches from popular favour. But, however keenly we may court such a death for ourselves or for those who are near and dear to us, we must always be offended whenever it befall one in whom our interest is æsthetic merely. Had his father permitted George to fight at Waterloo, and had some fatal bullet pierced the padding of that splendid breast, I should have been really annoyed, and this essay would never have been written. Sudden death mars the unity of an admirable life. Natural decline, tapering to tranquillity, is its proper end. As a man's life begins, faintly, and gives no token of childhood's intensity and the expansion of youth and the perfection of manhood, so it should also end, faintly. The King died a death that was like the calm conclusion of a great, lurid poem. *Quievit.*

Yes, his life was a poem, a poem in the praise of Pleasure. And it is right that we should think of him always as the great voluptuary. Only let us note that his nature never became, as do the natures of most voluptuaries, corroded by a cruel indifference to the happiness of others. When all the town was agog for the *fête* to be given by the Regent in honour of the

French King, Sheridan sent a forged card of invitation
to Romeo Coates, the half-witted dandy, who used at
this time to walk about in absurd ribbons and buckles,
and was the butt of all the streetsters. The poor fellow
arrived at the entrance of Carlton House, proud as a
peacock, and he was greeted with a tremendous cheer
from the bystanding mob, but when he came to the
lackeys he was told that his card was a hoax and sent
about his business. The tears were rolling down his
cheeks as he shambled back into the street. The Regent
heard later in the evening of this sorry joke, and next day
despatched a kindly-worded message, in which he prayed
that Mr. Coates would not refuse to come and ' view the
decorations, nevertheless.' Though he does not appear
to have treated his inferiors with the extreme servility
that is now in vogue, George was beloved by the whole
of his household, and many are the little tales that are
told to illustrate the kindliness and consideration he
showed to his valets and his jockeys and his stable-boys.
That from time to time he dropped certain of his
favourites is no cause for blaming him. Remember
that a Great Personage, like a great genius, is dangerous
to his fellow-creatures. The favourites of Royalty live
in an intoxicant atmosphere. They become unaccount-
able for their behaviour. Either they get beyond

themselves, and, like Brummell, forget that the King, their friend, is also their master, or they outrun the constable and go bankrupt, or cheat at cards in order to keep up their position, or do some other foolish thing that makes it impossible for the King to favour them more. Old friends are generally the refuge of unsociable persons. Remembering this also, gauge the temptation that besets the very leader of Society to form fresh friendships, when all the cleverest and most charming persons in the land are standing ready, like supers at the wings, to come on and please him ! At Carlton House there was a constant succession of wits. Minds were preserved for the Prince of Wales, as coverts are preserved for him to-day. For him Sheridan would flash his best bon-mot, and Theodore Hook play his most practical joke, his swiftest chansonette. And Fox would talk, as only he could, of Liberty and of Patriotism, and Byron would look more than ever like Isidore de Lara as he recited his own bad verses, and Sir Walter Scott would ' pour out with an endless generosity his store of old-world learning, kindness, and humour.' Of such men George was a splendid patron. He did not merely sit in his chair, gaping princely at their wit and their wisdom, but quoted with the scholars and argued with the statesmen and jested with

93

the wits. Doctor Burney, an impartial observer, says that he was amazed by the knowledge of music that the Regent displayed in a half-hour's discussion over the wine. Croker says that 'the Prince and Scott were the two most brilliant story-tellers, in their several ways, he had ever happened to meet. Both exerted themselves, and it was hard to say which shone the most.' Indeed His Royal Highness appears to have been a fine conversationalist, with a wide range of knowledge and great humour. We, who have come at length to look upon stupidity as one of the most sacred prerogatives of Royalty, can scarcely realise that, if George's birth had been never so humble, he would have been known to us as a most admirable scholar and wit, or as a connoisseur of the arts. It is pleasing to think of his love for the Flemish school of painting, for Wilkie and Sir Thomas Lawrence. The splendid portraits of foreign potentates that hang in the Banqueting Room at Windsor bear witness to his sense of the canvas. In his later years he exerted himself strenuously in raising the tone of the drama. His love of the classics never left him. We know he was fond of quoting those incomparable poets, Homer, at great length, and that he was prominent in the 'papyrus-craze.' Indeed, he inspired Society with a love of something more than mere pleasure, a love of the 'humaner delights.' He was a giver of tone. At his coming, the bluff, disgusting ways of the Tom and Jerry period gave way to those florid graces that are still called Georgian.

A pity that George's predecessor was not a man, like the Prince Consort, of strong chastening influence ! Then might the bright flamboyance which he gave to Society have made his reign more beautiful than any other—a real renaissance. But he found London a wild city of taverns and cock-pits, and the grace which in the course of years he gave to his subjects never really entered into them. The cock-pits were gilded and the taverns painted with colour, but the heart of the city was vulgar, even as before. The simulation of higher things did indeed give the note of a very interesting period, but how shallow that simulation was and how merely it was due to George's own influence, we may see in the light of what happened after his death. The good that he had done died with him. The refinement he had laid upon vulgarity fell away, like enamel from withered cheeks. It was only George himself who had made the sham endure. The Victorian era came soon, and the angels rushed in and drove the nymphs away and hung the land with reps.

I have often wondered whether it was with a feeling that his influence would be no more than life-long, that George allowed Carlton House, that dear structure, the very work of his life and symbol of his being, to be rased. I wish that Carlton House were still standing. I wish we could still walk through those corridors, whose walls were 'crusted with ormolu,' and parquet-floors were 'so glossy that, were Narcissus to come down from heaven, he would, I maintain, need no other mirror for his *beauté*.' I wish that we could see the pier-glasses and the girandoles and the twisted sofas, the fauns foisted upon the ceiling and the rident goddesses along the wall. These things would make George's memory dearer to us, help us to a fuller knowledge of him. I am glad that the Pavilion still stands here in Brighton. Its trite lawns and wanton cupolæ have taught me much. As I write this essay, I can see them from my window. Last night, in a crowd of trippers and townspeople, I roamed the lawns of that dishonoured palace, whilst a band played us tunes. Once I fancied I saw the shade of a swaying figure and of a wine-red face.

Brighton, 1894.

96

THE PERVASION OF ROUGE

Nay, but it is useless to protest. Artifice must queen it once more in the town, and so, if there be any whose hearts chafe at her return, let them not say, 'We have come into evil times,' and be all for resistance, reformation, or angry cavilling. For did the king's sceptre send the sea retrograde, or the wand of the sorcerer avail to turn the sun from its old course? And what man or what number of men ever stayed that inexorable process by which the cities of this world grow, are very strong, fail, and grow again? Indeed, indeed, there is charm in every period, and only fools and flutterpates do not seek reverently for what is charming in their own day. No martyrdom, however fine, nor satire, however splendidly bitter, has changed by a little tittle the known tendency of things. It is the times that can perfect us, not we the times, and so let all of us wisely acquiesce. Like the little wired marionettes, let us acquiesce in the dance.

For behold! The Victorian era comes to its end and the day of sancta simplicitas is quite ended. The old signs are here and the portents to warn the seer of life that we are ripe for a new epoch of artifice. Are not men rattling the dice-box and ladies dipping their fingers in the rouge-pot? At Rome, in the keenest time of her degringolade, when there was gambling even in the holy temples, great ladies (does not Lucian tell us?) did not scruple to squander all they had upon unguents from Arabia. Nero's mistress and unhappy wife, Poppæa, of shameful memory, had in her travelling retinue fifteen—or, as some say, fifty—she-asses, for the sake of their milk, that was thought an incomparable guard against cosmetics with poison in them. Last century, too, when life was lived by candle-light, and ethics was but etiquette, and even art a question of punctilio, women, we know, gave the best hours of the day to the crafty farding of their faces and the towering of their coiffures. And men, throwing passion into the wine-bowl to sink or swim, turned out thought to browse upon the green cloth. Cannot we even now in our fancy see them, those silent exquisites round the

long table at Brooks's, masked, all of them, 'lest the
countenance should betray feeling,' in quinze masks,
through whose eyelets they sat peeping, peeping, while
macao brought them riches or ruin ! We can see
them, those silent rascals, sitting there with their cards
and their rouleaux and their wooden money-bowls, long
after the dawn had crept up St. James's and pressed
its haggard face against the window of the little club.
Yes, we can raise their ghosts—and, more, we can see
manywhere a devotion to hazard fully as meek as theirs.
In England there has been a wonderful revival of cards.
Baccarat may rival dead faro in the tale of her devotees.
We have all seen the sweet English châtelaine at her
roulette wheel, and ere long it may be that tender
parents will be writing to complain of the compulsory
baccarat in our public schools.

In fact, we are all gamblers once more, but our
gambling is on a finer scale than ever it was. We fly
from the card-room to the heath, and from the heath
to the City, and from the City to the coast of the
Mediterranean. And just as no one seriously en-
courages the clergy in its frantic efforts to lay the
spirit of chance that has thus resurged among us, so no
longer are many faces set against that other great sign

of a more complicated life, the love for cosmetics. No longer is a lady of fashion blamed if, to escape the outrageous persecution of time, she fly for sanctuary to the toilet-table ; and if a damosel, prying in her mirror, be sure that with brush and pigment she can trick herself into more charm, we are not angry. Indeed, why should we ever have been ? Surely it is laudable, this wish to make fair the ugly and overtop fairness, and no wonder that within the last five years the trade of the makers of cosmetics has increased immoderately —twentyfold, so one of these makers has said to me. We need but walk down any modish street and peer into the little broughams that flit past, or (in Thackeray's phrase) under the bonnet of any woman we meet, to see over how wide a kingdom rouge reigns.

And now that the use of pigments is becoming general, and most women are not so young as they are painted, it may be asked curiously how the prejudice ever came into being. Indeed, it is hard to trace folly, for that it is inconsequent, to its start ; and perhaps it savours too much of reason to suggest that the prejudice was due to the tristful confusion man has made of soul and surface. Through trusting so keenly

to the detection of the one by keeping watch upon the
other, and by force of the thousand errors following,
he has come to think of surface even as the reverse of
soul. He seems to suppose that every clown beneath
his paint and lip-salve is moribund and knows it
(though in verity, I am told, clowns are as cheerful a
class of men as any other), that the fairer the fruit's
rind and the more delectable its bloom, the closer are
packed the ashes within it. The very jargon of the
hunting-field connects cunning with a mask. And so
perhaps came man's anger at the embellishment of
women—that lovely mask of enamel with its shadows
of pink and tiny pencilled veins, what must lurk
behind it? Of what treacherous mysteries may it not
be the screen? Does not the heathen lacquer her
dark face, and the harlot paint her cheeks, because
sorrow has made them pale?

After all, the old prejudice is a-dying. We need
not pry into the secret of its birth. Rather is this a
time of jolliness and glad indulgence. For the era of
rouge is upon us, and as only in an elaborate era can
man, by the tangled accrescency of his own pleasures
and emotions, reach that refinement which is his
highest excellence, and by making himself, so to say,

independent of Nature, come nearest to God, so only in an elaborate era is woman perfect. Artifice is the strength of the world, and in that same mask of paint and powder, shadowed with vermeil tinct and most trimly pencilled, is woman's strength.

For see ! We need not look so far back to see woman under the direct influence of Nature. Early in this century, our grandmothers, sickening of the odour of faded exotics and spilt wine, came out into the daylight once more and let the breezes blow around their faces and enter, sharp and welcome, into their lungs. Artifice they drove forth and they set Martin Tupper upon a throne of mahogany to rule over them. A very reign of terror set in. All things were sacrificed to the fetish Nature. Old ladies may still be heard to tell how, when they were girls, affectation was not ; and, if we verify their assertion in the light of such literary authorities as Dickens, we find that it is absolutely true. Women appear to have been in those days utterly natural in their conduct—flighty, fainting, blushing, gushing, giggling, and shaking their curls. They knew no reserve in the first days of the Victorian era. No thought was held too trivial, no emotion too silly, to express. To Nature everything was sacrificed.

Great heavens! And in those barren days what influence did women exert! By men they seem not to have been feared nor loved, but regarded rather as 'dear little creatures' or 'wonderful little beings,' and in their relation to life as foolish and ineffectual as the landscapes they did in water-colour. Yet, if the women of those years were of no great account, they had a certain charm, and they at least had not begun to trespass upon men's ground; if they touched not thought, which is theirs by right, at any rate they refrained from action, which is ours. Far more serious was it when, in the natural trend of time, they became enamoured of rinking and archery and galloping along the Brighton Parade. Swiftly they have sped on since then from horror to horror. The invasion of the tennis-courts and of the golf-links, the seizure of the bicycle and of the typewriter, were but steps pre-liminary in that campaign which is to end with the final victorious occupation of St. Stephen's. But stay! The horrific pioneers of womanhood who gad hither and thither and, confounding wisdom with the device on her shield, shriek for the unbecoming, are doomed. Though they spin their bicycle-treadles so amazingly fast, they are too late. Though they scream victory, none follow them. Artifice, that fair exile, has returned.

Yes, though the pioneers know it not, they are doomed already. For of the curiosities of history not the least strange is the manner in which two social movements may be seen to overlap, long after the second has, in truth, given its death-blow to the first. And, in like manner, as one has seen the limbs of a murdered thing in lively movement, so we need not doubt that, though the voices of those who cry out for reform be very terribly shrill, they will soon be hushed. Dear Artifice is with us. It needed but that we should wait.

Surely, without any of my pleading, women will welcome their great and amiable protectrix, as by instinct. For (have I not said?) it is upon her that all their strength, their life almost, depends. Artifice's first command to them is that they should repose. With bodily activity their powder will fly, their enamel crack. They are butterflies who must not flit, if they love their bloom. Now, setting aside the point of view of passion, from which very many obvious things might be said (and probably have been by the minor poets), it is, from the intellectual point of view, quite necessary that a woman should repose. Hers is the resupinate sex. On her couch she is a goddess, but so soon as ever she put her foot to the ground—lo, she is the veriest little sillypop, and quite done for. She cannot rival us in action, but she is our mistress in the things of the mind. Let her not by second-rate athletics, nor indeed by any exercise soever of the limbs, spoil the pretty procedure of her reason. Let her be content to remain the guide, the subtle suggester of what *we* must do, the strategist whose soldiers we are, the little architect whose workmen.

'After all,' as a pretty girl once said to me, 'women are a sex by themselves, so to speak,' and the sharper the line between their worldly functions and ours, the better. This greater swiftness and less erring subtlety of mind, their forte and privilege, justifies the painted mask that Artifice bids them wear. Behind it their minds can play without let. They gain the strength of reserve. They become important, as in the days of the Roman Empire were the Emperor's mistresses, as was the Pompadour at Versailles, as was our Elizabeth. Yet do not their faces become lined with thought; beautiful and without meaning are their faces.

And, truly, of all the good things that will happen

with the full revival of cosmetics, one of the best is
that surface will finally be severed from soul. That
damnable confusion will be solved by the extinguishing
of a prejudice which, as I suggest, itself created. Too
long has the face been degraded from its rank as a
thing of beauty to a mere vulgar index of character
or emotion. We had come to troubling ourselves, not
with its charm of colour and line, but with such questions as whether the lips were sensuous, the eyes full
of sadness, the nose indicative of determination. I
have no quarrel with physiognomy. For my own part
I believe in it. But it has tended to degrade the face
æsthetically, in such wise as the study of cheirosophy
has tended to degrade the hand. And the use of
cosmetics, the masking of the face, will change this.
We shall gaze at a woman merely because she is beautiful, not stare into her face anxiously, as into the face
of a barometer.

How fatal it has been, in how many ways, this confusion of soul and service! Wise were the Greeks
in making plain masks for their mummers to play in,
and dunces we not to have done the same! Only the
other day, an actress was saying that what she was
most proud of in her art—next, of course, to having

appeared in some provincial pantomime at the age of three—was the deftness with which she contrived, in parts demanding a rapid succession of emotions, to dab her cheeks quite quickly with rouge from the palm of her right hand or powder from the palm of her left. Gracious goodness ! why do not we have masks upon the stage ? Drama is the presentment of the soul in action. The mirror of the soul is the voice. Let the young critics, who seek a cheap reputation for austerity, by cavilling at ' incidental music,' set their faces rather against the attempt to justify inferior dramatic art by the subvention of a quite alien art like painting, of any art, indeed, whose sphere is only surface. Let those, again, who sneer, so rightly, at the ' painted anecdotes of the Academy,' censure equally the writers who trespass on painters' ground. It is a proclaimed sin that a painter should concern himself with a good little girl's affection for a Scotch grey-hound, or the keen enjoyment of their port by elderly gentlemen of the early 'forties. Yet, for a painter to prod the soul with his paint-brush is no worse than for a novelist to refuse to dip under the surface, and the fashion of avoiding a psychological study of grief by stating that the owner's hair turned white in a single night, or of shame by mentioning a sudden rush of scarlet to the cheeks, is as lamentable as may be. But ! But with the universal use of cosmetics and the consequent secernment of soul and surface, upon which, at the risk of irritating a reader, I must again insist, all those old properties that went to bolster up the ordinary novel—the trembling lips, the flashing eyes, the determined curve of the chin, the nervous trick of biting the moustache, aye, and the hectic spot of red on either cheek—will be made spiflicate, as the puppets were spiflicated by Don Quixote. Yes, even now Demos begins to discern. The same spirit that has revived rouge, smote his mouth as it grinned at the wondrous painter of mist and river, and now sends him sprawling for the pearls that Meredith dived for in the deep waters of romance.

Indeed the revival of cosmetics must needs be so splendid an influence, conjuring boons innumerable, that one inclines almost to mutter against that inexorable law by which Artifice must perish from time to time. That such branches of painting as the staining of glass or the illuminating of manuscripts should fall into disuse seems, in comparison, so likely ; these were esoteric arts ; they died with the monastic spirit. But

personal appearance is art's very basis. The painting
of the face is the first kind of painting men can have
known. To make beautiful things—is it not an im-
pulse laid upon few ? But to make oneself beautiful
is an universal instinct. Strange that the resultant art
could ever perish ! So fascinating an art too ! So
various in its materials from stimmis, psimythium, and
fuligo to bismuth and arsenic, so simple in that its
ground and its subject-matter are one, so marvellous in
that its very subject-matter becomes lovely when an
artist has selected it ! For surely this is no idle nor
fantastic saying. To deny that 'making up' is an art,
on the pretext that the finished work of its exponents
depends for beauty and excellence upon the ground
chosen for the work, is absurd. At the touch of a true
artist, the plainest face turns comely. As subject-
matter the face is no more than suggestive, as ground,
merely a loom round which the beatus artifex may spin
the threads of any golden fabric :

> *Quae nunc nomen habent operosi signa Maronis*
> *Pondus iners quondam duraque massa fuit.*
> *Multa viros nescire decet ; pars maxima rerum*
> *Offendat, si non interiora tegas,*

and, as Ovid would seem to suggest, by pigments any

tone may be set aglow on a woman's cheek, from enamel the features take any form. Insomuch that surely the advocates of soup-kitchens and free-libraries and other devices for giving people what Providence did not mean them to receive should send out pamphlets in the praise of self-embellishment. For it will place Beauty within easy reach of many who could not otherwise hope to attain to it.

But of course Artifice is rather exacting. In return for the repose she forces—so wisely !—upon her followers when the sun is high or the moon is blown across heaven, she demands that they should pay her long homage at the sun's rising. The initiate may not enter lightly upon her mysteries. For, if a bad complexion be inexcusable, to be ill-painted is unforgivable ; and, when the toilet is laden once more with the fulness of its elaboration, we shall hear no more of the proper occupation for women. And think, how sweet an energy, to sit at the mirror of coquetry ! See the dear merits of the toilet as shown upon old vases, or upon the walls of Roman ruins, or, rather still, read Böttiger's alluring, scholarly description of 'Morgenscenen im Puttzimmer Einer Reichen Römerin.' Read of Sabina's face as she comes through the curtain of her bed-chamber to the chamber of her toilet. The slave-girls have long been chafing their white feet upon the marble floor. They stand, those timid Greek girls, marshalled in little battalions. Each has her appointed task, and all kneel in welcome as Sabina stalks, ugly and frowning, to the toilet chair. Scaphion steps forth from among them, and, dipping a tiny sponge in a bowl of hot milk, passes it lightly, ever so lightly, over her mistress' face. The Poppæan pastes melt beneath it like snow. A cooling lotion is poured over her brow, and is fanned with feathers. Phiale comes after, a clever girl, captured in some sea-skirmish on the Ægean. In her left hand she holds the ivory box wherein are the phucus and that white powder, psimy-thium; in her right a sheaf of slim brushes. With how sure a touch does she mingle the colours, and in what sweet proportion blushes and blanches her lady's upturned face. Phiale is the cleverest of all the slaves. Now Calamis dips her quill in a certain powder that floats, liquid and sable, in the hollow of her palm. Standing upon tip-toe and with lips parted, she traces the arch of the eyebrows. The slaves whisper loudly of their lady's beauty, and two of them hold up a mirror to her. Yes, the eyebrows are rightly arched.

But why does Psecas abase herself? She is craving
leave to powder Sabina's hair with a fine new powder.
It is made of the grated rind of the cedar-tree, and a
Gallic perfumer, whose stall is near the Circus, gave it
to her for a kiss. No lady in Rome knows of it. And
so, when four special slaves have piled up the head-
dress, out of a perforated box this glistening powder is
showered. Into every little brown ringlet it enters,
till Sabina's hair seems like a pile of gold coins. Lest
the breezes send it flying, the girls lay the powder with
sprinkled attar. Soon Sabina will start for the Temple
of Cybele.

Ah! Such are the lures of the toilet that none will
for long hold aloof from them. Cosmetics are not
going to be a mere prosaic remedy for age or plainness,
but all ladies and all young girls will come to love them.
Does not a certain blithe Marquise, whose *lettres intimes*
from the Court of Louis Seize are less read than their
wit deserves, tell us how she was scandalised to see
'*même les toutes jeunes demoiselles émaillées comme ma
tabatière*'? So it shall be with us. Surely the common
prejudice against painting the lily can but be based on
mere ground of economy. That which is already fair
is complete, it may be urged—urged implausibly, for

there are not so many lovely things in this world that
we can afford not to know each one of them by heart.
There is only one white lily, and who that has ever
seen—as I have—a lily really well painted could grudge
the artist so fair a ground for his skill ? Scarcely do
you believe through how many nice metamorphoses a
lily may be passed by him. In like manner, we all
know the young girl, with her simpleness, her goodness, her wayward ignorance. And a very charming
ideal for England must she have been, and a very
natural one, when a young girl sat even on the throne.
But no nation can keep its ideal for ever, and it needed
none of Mr. Gilbert's delicate satire in 'Utopia' to
remind us that she had passed out of our ken with the
rest of the early Victorian era. What writer of plays,
as lately asked some pressman, who had been told off to
attend many first nights and knew what he was talking
about, ever dreams of making the young girl the centre
of his theme ? Rather he seeks inspiration from the
tried and tired woman of the world, in all her intricate
maturity, whilst, by way of comic relief, he sends the
young girl flitting in and out with a tennis-racket, the
poor εἴδωλον ἀμαυρόν of her former self. The season
of the unsophisticated is gone by, and the young girl's

final extinction beneath the rising tides of cosmetics will leave no gap in life and will rob art of nothing.

'Tush,' I can hear some damned flutterpate exclaim, 'girlishness and innocence are as strong and as permanent as womanhood itself! Why, a few months past, the whole town went mad over Miss Cissie Loftus! Was not hers a success of girlish innocence and the absence of rouge? If such things as these be outmoded, why was she so wildly popular?' Indeed, the triumph of that clever girl, whose *début* made London nice even in August, is but another witness to the truth of my contention. In a very sophisticated time, simplicity has a new dulcedo. Hers was a success of contrast. Accustomed to clever malaperts like Miss Lloyd or Miss Reeve, whose experienced pouts and smiles under the sun-bonnet are a standing burlesque of innocence and girlishness, Demos was really delighted, for once and away, to see the real presentment of these things upon his stage. Coming after all those sly serios, coming so young and mere with her pink frock and straightly combed hair, Miss Cissie Loftus had the charm which things of another period often do possess. Besides, just as we adored her for the abrupt nod with which she was wont at first to acknowledge the applause, so we were glad for her to come upon the stage with nothing to tinge the ivory of her cheeks. It seemed so strange, that neglect of convention. To be behind footlights and not rouged ! Yes, hers was a success of contrast. She was like a daisy in the window at Solomons'. She was delightful. And yet, such is the force of convention, that when last I saw her, playing in some burlesque at the Gaiety, her fringe was curled and her pretty face rouged with the best of them. And, if further need be to show the absurdity of having called her performance ' a triumph of naturalness over the jaded spirit of modernity,' let us reflect that the little mimic was not a real old-fashioned girl after all. She had none of that restless naturalness that would seem to have characterised the girl of the early Victorian days. She had no pretty ways— no smiles nor blushes nor tremors. Possibly Demos could not have stood a presentment of girlishness unrestrained.

But, with her grave insouciance, Miss Cissie Loftus had much of the reserve that is one of the factors of feminine perfection, and to most comes only, as I have said, with artifice. Her features played very, very slightly. And in truth, this may have been one of the reasons of her great success. For expression is but too often the ruin of a face; and, since we cannot, as yet, so order the circumstances of life that women shall never be betrayed into 'an unbecoming emotion,' when the brunette shall never have cause to blush nor La Gioconda to frown, the safest way by far is to create, by brush and pigments, artificial expression for every face.

And this—say you ?—will make monotony ? You are mistaken, *toto cœlo* mistaken. When your mistress has wearied you with one expression, then it will need but a few touches of that pencil, a backward sweep of that brush, and lo, you will bê revelling in another. For though, of course, the painting of the face is, in manner, most like the painting of canvas, in outcome it is rather akin to the art of music—lasting, like music's echo, not for very long. So that, no doubt, of the many little appurtenances of the Reformed Toilet Table, not the least vital will be a list of the emotions that become its owner, with recipes for simulating them. According to the colour she wills her hair to be for the time—black or yellow or, peradventure, burnished red—she will blush for you, sneer for you, laugh or languish for you. The good combinations of line and colour are nearly numberless, and by their means poor restless woman will be able to realise her moods in all their shades and lights and dappledoms, to live many lives and masquerade through many moments of joy. No monotony will be. And for us men matrimony will have lost its sting.

But that in the world of women they will not neglect this art, so ripping in itself, in its result so wonderfully beneficent, I am sure indeed. Much, I have said, is already done for its full revival. The spirit of the age has made straight the path of its professors. Fashion has made Jezebel surrender her monopoly of the rouge-pot. As yet, the great art of self-embellishment is for us but in its infancy. But if Englishwomen can bring it to the flower of an excellence so supreme as never yet has it known, then, though Old England lose her martial and commercial supremacy, we patriots wil have the satisfaction of knowing that she has been advanced at one bound to a place in the councils of æsthetic Europe. And, in sooth, is this hoping too high of my countrywomen ? True that, as the art seems always to have appealed to the ladies of Athens, and it was not until the waning time of the Republic that Roman ladies learned to love the practice of it, so

Paris, Athenian in this as in all other things, has been
noted hitherto as a far more vivid centre of the art than
London.   But it was in Rome, under the Emperors,
that unguentaria reached its zenith, and shall it not be
in London, soon, that unguentaria shall outstrip its
Roman   perfection !   Surely   there   must   be   among
us artists as cunning in the use of brush and puff as
any who lived at Versailles.   Surely the splendid, impalpable advance of good taste, as shown in dress and
in the decoration of houses, may justify my hope of the
preëminence of Englishwomen in the cosmetic   art.
By their innate delicacy of touch they will accomplish
much, and much, of course, by their swift feminine
perception.   Yet it were well that they should know
something also of the theoretical side of the craft.
Modern authorities upon the mysteries of the toilet are,
it is true, rather few ; but among the ancients many
a writer would seem to have been fascinated by them.
Archigenes, a man of science at the Court of Cleopatra,
and Criton at the Court of the Emperor Trajan, both
wrote treatises upon cosmetics—doubtless most scholarly
treatises that would have given many a precious hint.
It is a pity they are not extant.   From Lucian or from
Juvenal, with his bitter picture of a Roman *levée*, much

may be learnt ; from the staid pages of Xenophon and
Aristophanes' dear farces. But best of all is that fine
book of the Ars Amatoria that Ovid has set aside
for the consideration of dyes, perfumes, and pomades.
Written by an artist who knew the allurement of the
toilet and understood its philosophy, it remains without
rival as a treatise upon Artifice. It is more than a
poem, it is a manual ; and if there be left in England
any lady who cannot read Latin in the original, she
will do well to procure a discreet translation. In the
Bodleian Library there is treasured the only known
copy of a very poignant and delightful rendering of this
one book of Ovid's masterpiece. It was made by a
certain Wye Waltonstall, who lived in the days of
Elizabeth, and, seeing that he dedicated it to 'the
Vertuous Ladyes and Gentlewomen of Great Britain,'
I am sure that the gallant writer, could he know of our
great renaissance of cosmetics, would wish his little
work to be placed once more within their reach.
'Inafmuch as to you, ladyes and gentlewomen,' so he
writes in his queer little dedication, 'my booke of
pigments doth firft addreffe itfelf, that it may kifle
your hands and afterward have the lines thereof in
reading fweetened by the odour of your breath, while

the dead letters formed into words by your divided lips
may receive new life by your paffionate expreffion, and
the words marryed in that Ruby coloured temple may
thus happily united, multiply your contentment.' It
is rather sad to think that, at this crisis in the history
of pigments, the Vertuous Ladyes and Gentlewomen
cannot read the libellus of Wye Waltonstall, who did
so dearly love pigments.

But since the days when these great critics wrote
their treatises, with what gifts innumerable has Artifice
been loaded by Science ! Many little partitions must
be added to the narthecium before it can comprehend
all the new cosmetics that have been quietly devised
since classical days, and will make the modern toilet
chalks away more splendid in its possibilities. A pity
that no one has devoted himself to the compiling of a
new list ; but doubtless all the newest devices are
known to the admirable unguentarians of Bond Street,
who will impart them to their clients. Our thanks,
too, should be given to Science for ridding us of the
old danger that was latent in the use of cosmetics.
Nowadays they cannot, being purged of any poisonous
element, do harm to the skin that they make beautiful.
There need be no more sowing the seeds of destruction

in the furrows of time, no martyrs to the cause like Maria, Countess of Coventry, that fair dame but infelix, who died, so they relate, from the effect of a poisonous rouge upon her lips. No, we need have no fears now. Artifice will claim not another victim from among her worshippers.

Loveliness shall sit at the toilet, watching her oval face in the oval mirror. Her smooth fingers shall flit among the paints and powder, to tip and mingle them, catch up a pencil, clasp a phial, and what not and what *not*, until the mask of vermeil tint has been laid aptly, the enamel quite hardened. And, heavens, how she will charm us and ensorcel our eyes! Positively rouge will rob us for a time of all our reason; we shall go mad over masks. Was it not at Capua that they had a whole street where nothing was sold but dyes and unguents? We must have such a street, and, to fill our new Seplasia, our Arcade of the Unguents, all herbs and minerals and live creatures shall give of their substance. The white cliffs of Albion shall be ground to powder for Loveliness, and perfumed by the ghost of many a little violet. The fluffy eider-ducks, that are swimming round the pond, shall lose their feathers, that the powder-puff may be moonlike as it passes over

Loveliness' lovely face. Even the camels shall become ministers of delight, giving many tufts of their hair to be stained in her splendid colour-box, and across her cheek the swift hare's foot shall fly as of old. The sea shall offer her the phucus, its scarlet weed. We shall spill the blood of mulberries at her bidding. And, as in another period of great ecstasy, a dancing wanton, la belle Aubrey, was crowned upon a church's lighted altar, so Arsenic, that ' greentress'd goddess,' ashamed at length of skulking between the soup of the unpopular and the test-tubes of the Queen's analyst, shall be exalted to a place of consummate honour upon the toilet-table of Loveliness.

All these things shall come to pass. Times of jolliness and glad indulgence ! For Artifice, whom we drove forth, has returned among us, and, though her eyes are red with crying, she is smiling forgiveness. She is kind. Let us dance and be glad, and trip the cockawhoop ! Artifice, sweetest exile, is come into her kingdom. Let us dance her a welcome !

Oxford, 1894.

POOR ROMEO!

Even now Bath glories in his legend, not idly, for he was the most fantastic animal that ever stepped upon her pavement. Were ever a statue given him (and indeed he is worthy of a grotesque in marble), it would be put in Pulteney Street or the Circus. I know that the palm trees of Antigua overshadowed his cradle, that there must be even now in Boulogne many who set eyes on him in the time of his less fatuous declension, that he died in London. But Mr. Coates (for of that Romeo I write) must be claimed by none of these places. Bath saw the laughable disaster of his *début*, and so, in a manner, his whole life seems to belong to her, and the story of it to be a part of her annals.

The Antiguan was already on the brink of middle-age when he first trod the English shore. But, for all his thirty-seven years, he had the heart of a youth, and his purse being yet as heavy as his heart was light, the English sun seemed to shine gloriously about his path and gild the letters of introduction that he scattered everywhere. Also, he was a gentleman of amiable, nearly elegant mien, and something of a scholar. His father had been the most respectable resident Antigua could show, so that little Robert, the future Romeo, had often sat at dessert with distinguished travellers through the Indies. But in the year 1807 old Mr. Coates had died. As we may read in vol. lxxviii. of *The Gentleman's Magazine*, ' the Almighty, whom he alone feared, was pleased to take him from this life, after having sustained an untarnished reputation for seventy-three years,' a passage which, though objectionable in its theology, gives the true story of Romeo's antecedents and disposes of the later calumnies that declared him the son of a tailor. Realising that he was now an orphan, an orphan with not a few grey hairs, our hero had set sail in quest of amusing adventure.

For three months he took the waters of Bath, unobtrusively, like other well-bred visitors. His attendance was solicited for all the most fashionable routs, and at assemblies he sat always in the shade of some titled turban. In fact, Mr. Coates was a great success. There was an air of most romantic mystery that endeared his presence to all the damsels fluttering fans in the Pump Room. It set them vying for his conduct through the mazes of the Quadrille or of the Triumph, and blushing at the sound of his name. Alas! their tremulous rivalry lasted not long. Soon they saw that Emma, sole daughter of Sir James Tylney Long, that wealthy baronet, had cast a magic net about the warm Antiguan heart. In the wake of her chair, by night and day, Mr. Coates was obsequious. When she cried that she would not drink the water without some delicacy to banish the iron taste, it was he who stood by with a box of vanilla-rusks. When he shaved his great moustachio, it was at her caprice. And his devotion to Miss Emma was the more noted for that his own considerable riches were proof that it was true and single. He himself warned her, in some verses written for him by Euphemia Boswell, against the crew of penniless admirers who surrounded her :

> *Lady, ah ! too bewitching lady ! now beware*
> *Of artful men that fain would thee ensnare*
> *Not for thy merit, but thy fortune's sake.*
> *Give me your hand—your cash let venals take.'*

I

Miss Emma was his first love. To understand his subsequent behaviour, let us remember that Cupid's shaft pierces most poignantly the breast of middle-age. Not that Mr. Coates was laughed at in Bath for a love-a-lack-a-daisy. On the contrary, his mien, his manner, were as yet so studiously correct, his speech so reticent, that laughter had been unusually inept. The only strange taste evinced by him was his devotion to theatricals. He would hold forth, by the hour, upon the fine conception of such parts as Macbeth, Othello and, especially, Romeo. Many ladies and gentlemen were privileged to hear him recite, in this or that drawing-room, after supper. All testified to the real fire with which he inflamed the lines of love or hatred. His voice, his gesture, his scholarship, were all approved. A fine symphony of praise assured Mr. Coates that no suitor worthier than he had ever courted Thespis. The lust for the footlights' glare grew lurid in his mothish eye. What, after all, were these poor triumphs of the parlour ? It might be that contemptuous Emma, hearing the loud salvos of the gallery and boxes, would call him at length her lord.

At this time there arrived at the York House Mr.

Pryse Gordon, whose memoirs we know. Mr. Coates himself was staying at number ** Gay Street, but was in the habit of breakfasting daily at the York House, where he attracted Mr. Gordon's attention by 'rehearsing passages from Shakespeare, with a tone and gesture extremely striking both to the eye and the ear.' Mr. Gordon warmly complimented him and suggested that he should give a public exposition of his art. The cheeks of the amateur flushed with pleasure. 'I am ready and willing,' he replied, 'to play "Romeo" to a Bath audience, if the manager will get up the play and give me a good "Juliet"; my costume is superb and adorned with diamonds, but I have not the advantage of knowing the manager, Dimonds.' Pleased by the stranger's ready wit, Mr. Gordon scribbled a note of introduction to Dimonds there and then. So soon as he had 'discussed a brace of muffins and so many eggs,' the new Romeo started for the playhouse, and that very day bills were posted to the effect that 'a Gentleman of Fashion would make his first appearance on February 9 in a *rôle* of Shakespeare.' All the lower boxes were immediately secured by Lady Belmore and other lights of Bath. 'Butlers and Abigails,' it is said, 'were commanded by their mistresses to take their stand in the centre of the pit and give Mr. Coates a capital, hearty clapping.' Indeed, throughout the week that elapsed before the *première*, no pains were spared in assuring a great success. Miss Tylney Long showed some interest in the arrangements. Gossip spoke of her as a likely bride.

The night came. Fashion, Virtue, and Intellect thronged the house. Nothing could have been more cordial than the temper of the gallery. All were eager to applaud the new Romeo. Presently, when the varlets of Verona had brawled, there stepped into the square—what !—a mountebank, a monstrosity. Hurrah died upon every lip. The house was thunderstruck. Whose legs were in those scarlet pantaloons ? Whose face grinned over that bolster-cravat, and under that Charles II. wig and opera-hat ? From whose shoulders hung that spangled sky-blue cloak ? Was this bedizened scarecrow the Amateur of Fashion, for sight of whom they had paid their shillings ? At length a voice from the gallery cried, 'Good evening, Mr. Coates,' and, as the Antiguan—for he it was—bowed low, the theatre was filled with yells of merriment. Only the people in the boxes were still silent, staring coldly at the *protégé* who had played them so odious a prank. Lady

Belmore rose and called for her chariot. Her example was followed by several ladies of rank. The rest sat spellbound, and of their number was Miss Tylney Long, at whose rigid face many glasses were, of course, directed. Meanwhile the play proceeded. Those lines that were not drowned in laughter Mr. Coates spoke in the most foolish and extravagant manner. He cut little capers at odd moments. He laid his hand on his heart and bowed, now to this, now to that part of the house, always with a grin. In the balcony-scene he produced a snuff-box, and, after taking a pinch, offered it to the bewildered Juliet. Coming down to the footlights, he laid it on the cushion of the stage-box and begged the inmates to refresh themselves, and to ' pass the golden trifle on.' The performance, so obviously grotesque, was just the kind of thing to please the gods. The limp of Hephaestus could not have called laughter so unquenchable from their lips. It is no trifle to set Englishmen laughing, but once you have done it, you can hardly stop them. Act after act of the beautiful love-play was performed without one sign of satiety from the seers of it. The laughter rather swelled in volume. Romeo died in so ludicrous a way that a cry of ' encore ' arose and the death was actually twice repeated. At the fall of the curtain there was prolonged applause. Mr. Coates came forward, and the good-humoured public pelted him with fragments of the benches. One splinter struck his right temple, inflicting a scar, of which Mr. Coates was, in his old age, not a little proud. Such is the traditional account of this curious *début*. Mr. Pryse Gordon, however, in his memoirs tells another tale. He professes to have seen nothing peculiar in Romeo's dress, save its display of fine diamonds, and to have admired the whole interpretation. The attitude of the audience he attributes to a hostile cabal. John R. and Hunter H. Robinson, in their memoir of Romeo Coates, echo Mr. Pryse Gordon's tale. They would have done well to weigh their authorities more accurately.

I had often wondered at this discrepancy between document and tradition. Last spring, when I was in Bath for a few days, my mind brooded especially on the question. Indeed, Bath, with her faded memories, her *tristesse*, drives one to reverie. Fashion no longer smiles from her windows nor dances in her sunshine, and in her deserted parks the invalids build up their constitutions. Now and again, as one of the frequent chairs glided past me, I wondered if its shadowy freight were the ghost of poor Romeo. I felt sure that the traditional account of his *début* was mainly correct. How could it, indeed, be false? Tradition is always a safer guide to truth than is the tale of one man. I might amuse myself here, in Bath, by verifying my notion of the *début* or proving it false.

One morning I was walking through a narrow street in the western quarter of Bath, and came to the window of a very little shop, which was full of dusty books, prints and engravings. I spied in one corner of it the discoloured print of a queer, lean figure, posturing in a garden. In one hand this figure held a snuff-box, in the other an opera-hat. Its sharp features and wide grin, flanked by luxuriant whiskers, looked strange under a Caroline wig. Above it was a balcony and a lady in an attitude of surprise. Beneath it were these words, faintly lettered : *Bombastes Coates wooing the Peerless Capulet, that's 'nough (that snuff)* 1809. I coveted the print. I went into the shop.

A very old man peered at me and asked my errand. I pointed to the print of Mr. Coates, which he gave me for a few shillings, chuckling at the pun upon the margin.

'Ah,' he said, 'they're forgetting him now, but he was a fine figure, a fine sort of figure.'

'You saw him ?'

'No, no. I'm only seventy. But I've known those who saw him. My father had a pile of such prints.'

'Did your father see him ?' I asked, as the old man furled my treasure and tied it with a piece of tape.

'My father, sir, was a friend of Mr. Coates,' he said. 'He entertained him in Gay Street. Mr. Coates was my father's lodger all the months he was in Bath. A good tenant, too. Never eccentric under my father's roof—never eccentric.'

I begged the old bookseller to tell me more of this matter. It seemed that his father had been a citizen of some consequence, and had owned a house in modish Gay Street, where he let lodgings. Thither, by the advice of a friend, Mr. Coates had gone so soon as he arrived in the town, and had stayed there down to the day after his *début*, when he left for London.

'My father often told me that Mr. Coates was crying bitterly when he settled the bill and got into his travelling-chaise. He'd come back from the play-house the night before as cheerful as could be. He'd said *he* didn't mind what the public thought of his act-

136

ing. But in the morning a letter was brought for him, and when he read it he seemed to go quite mad.'

'I wonder what was in the letter !' I asked. 'Did your father never know who sent it ?'

'Ah,' my greybeard rejoined, 'that's the most curious thing. And it's a secret. I can't tell you.'

He was not as good as his word. I bribed him delicately with the purchase of more than one old book. Also, I think, he was flattered by my eager curiosity to learn his long-pent secret. He told me that the 'letter was brought to the house by one of the footmen of Sir James Tylney Long, and that his father himself delivered it into the hands of Mr Coates.

'When he had read it through, the poor gentleman tore it into many fragments, and stood staring before him, pale as a ghost. " I must not stay another hour in Bath," he said. When he was gone, my father (God forgive him !) gathered up all the scraps of the letter, and for a long time he tried to piece them together. But there were a great many of them, and my father was not a scholar, though he was affluent.'

'What became of the scraps ?' I asked. 'Did your father keep them ?'

'Yes, he did. And I used to try, when I was

137

younger, to make out something from them. But
even I never seemed to get near it. I've never thrown
them away, though. They're in a box.'

I got them for a piece of gold that I could ill spare
—some score or so of shreds of yellow paper, traversed
with pale ink. The joy of the archæologist with an
unknown papyrus, of the detective with a clue, surged
in me. Indeed, I was not sure whether I was engaged
in private inquiry or in research; so recent, so remote
was the mystery. After two days' labour, I marshalled
the elusive words. This is the text of them :

Mr. Coates, Sir,

They say Revenge is sweet. I am fortunate to find it is
so. I have compelled you to be far more a Fool than you made me
at the *fête-champêtre* of Lady B. & I, having accomplished my aim,
am ready to forgive you now, as you implored me on the occasion
of the *fête*. But pray build no Hope that I, forgiving you, will
once more regard you as my Suitor. For that cannot ever be. I
decided you should show yourself a Fool before many people. But
such Folly does not commend your hand to mine. Therefore desist
your irksome attention &, if need be, begone from Bath. I have
punished you, & would save my eyes the *trouble* to turn away from
your person. I pray that you regard this epistle as privileged and
private.

E. T. L.   10 of February.

The letter lies before me as I write. It is written throughout in a firm and very delicate Italian hand. Under the neat initials is drawn, instead of the ordinary flourish, an arrow, and the absence of any erasure in a letter of such moment suggests a calm, deliberate character and, probably, rough copies. I did not, at the time, suffer my fancy to linger over the tessellated document. I set to elucidating the reference to the *fête-champêtre*. As I retraced my footsteps to the little bookshop, I wondered if I should find any excuse for the cruel faithlessness of Emma Tylney Long.

The bookseller was greatly excited when I told him I had re-created the letter. He was very eager to see it. I did not pander to his curiosity. He even offered to buy the article back at cost price. I asked him if he had ever heard, in his youth, of any scene that had passed between Miss Tylney Long and Mr. Coates at some *fête-champêtre*. The old man thought for some time, but he could not help me. Where then, I asked him, could I search old files of local newspapers? He told me that there were supposed to be many such files mouldering in the archives of the Town Hall.

I secured access, without difficulty, to these files.

A whole day I spent in searching the copies issued by
this and that journal during the months that Romeo
was in Bath. In the yellow pages of these forgotten
prints I came upon many complimentary allusions to
Mr. Coates : 'The visitor welcomed (by all our
aristocracy) from distant Ind,' 'the ubiquitous,' 'the
charitable *riche*.' Of his 'forthcoming impersonation
of Romeo and Juliet' there were constant puffs, quite
in the modern manner. The accounts of his *début* all
showed that Mr. Pryse Gordon's account of it was
fabulous. In one paper there was a bitter attack on
'Mr. Gordon, who was responsible for this insult to
Thespian art, the gentry, and the people, for he first
arranged the *whole production*'—an extract which makes
it clear that this gentleman had a good motive for his
version of the affair.

But I began to despair of ever learning what
happened at the *fête-champêtre*. There were accounts
of 'a grand garden-party, whereto Lady Belper, on
March the twenty-eighth, invited a host of fashionable
persons.' The names of Mr. Coates and of 'Sir
James Tylney Long and his daughter' were duly
recorded in the lists. But that was all. I turned at
length to a tiny file, consisting of five copies only,

Bladud's Courier. Therein I found this paragraph, followed by some scurrilities which I will not quote:

'Mr. C**t*s, who will act Romeo (*Wherefore art thou Romeo?*) this coming week for the pleasure of *his fashionable circle,* incurred the contemptuous wrath of his Lady Fair at the Fête. It was a sad pity she entrusted him to hold her purse while she fed the gold-fishes. He was very proud of the honour till the gold fell from his hand among the gold-fishes. How appropriate was the misadventure! But Miss Black Eyes, angry at her loss and her swain's clumsiness, cried: "Jump into the pond, sir, and find my purse *instanter!*" Several wags encouraged her, and the ladies were of the opinion that her adorer should certainly dive for the treasure. "Alas," the fellow said, "I cannot swim, Miss. But tell me how many guineas you carried and I will make them good to yourself." There was a great deal of laughter at this encounter, and *the haughty damsel turned on her heel,* nor did she vouchsafe another word to her *elderly* lover.

> 'When recreant man
> Meets lady's wrath, &c. &c.'

So the story of the *début* was complete! Was ever a lady more inexorable, more ingenious, in her revenge? One can fancy the poor Antiguan going to the Baronet's house next day with a bouquet of flowers and passionately abasing himself, craving her forgiveness. One can fancy the wounded vanity of the girl, her shame that people had mocked her for the disobedience of her suitor. Revenge, as her letter shows, became her one thought. She would strike him through his other love, the love of Thespis. ' I have compelled you,' she wrote afterwards, in her bitter triumph, ' to be a greater Fool than you made me.' She, then, it was that drove him to his public absurdity, she who insisted that he should never win her unless he sacrificed his dear longing for stage-laurels and actually pilloried himself upon the stage. The wig, the pantaloons, the snuff-box, the grin, were all conceived, I fancy, in her pitiless spite. It is possible that she did but say : ' The more ridiculous you make yourself, the more hope for you.' But I do not believe that Mr. Coates, a man of no humour, conceived the means himself. *They* were surely hers.

It is terrible to think of the ambitious amateur in his bedroom, secretly practising hideous antics or gazing at his absurd apparel before a mirror. How loath must he have been to desecrate the lines he loved so dearly and had longed to declaim in all their beauty and their resonance ! And then, what irony at the daily rehearsal ! With how sad a smile must he have received the compliments of Mr. Dimonds on his fine performance, knowing how different it would all be ' on the night ! ' Nothing could have steeled him to the ordeal but his great love. He must have wavered, had not the exaltation of his love protected him. But the jeers of the mob were music in his hearing, his wounds love-symbols. Then came the girl's cruel contempt of his martyrdom.

Aphrodite, who has care of lovers, did not spare Miss Tylney Long. She made her love, a few months after, one who married her for her fortune and broke her heart. In years of misery the wayward girl worked out the penance of her unpardonable sin, dying, at length, in poverty and despair. Into the wounds of him who had so truly loved her was poured, after a space of fourteen years, the balsam of another love. On the 6th September 1823, at St. George's, Hanover Square, Mr. Coates was married to Miss Anne Robinson, who was a faithful and devoted wife to him till he died.

Meanwhile, the rejected Romeo did not long repine. Two months after the tragedy at Bath, he was at Brighton, mingling with all the fashionable folk, and giving admirable recitations at routs. He was seen every day on the Parade, attired in an extravagant manner, very different to that he had adopted in Bath.

A pale-blue *surtout*, tasselled Hessians, and a cocked
hat were the most obvious items of his costume. He
also affected a very curious tumbril, shaped like a shell
and richly gilded. In this he used to drive around,
every afternoon, amid the gapes of the populace. It
is evident that, once having tasted the fruit of noto-
riety, he was loath to fall back on simpler fare. He
had become a prey to the love of absurd ostentation.
A lively example of dandyism unrestrained by taste,
he parodied in his person the foibles of Mr. Brummell
and the King. His diamonds and his equipage and
other follies became the gossip of every newspaper in
England. Nor did a day pass without the publication
of some little rigmarole from his pen. Wherever there
was a vacant theatre—were it in Cheltenham, Birming-
ham, or any other town—he would engage it for his
productions. One night he would play his favourite
part, Romeo, with reverence and ability. The next,
he would repeat his first travesty in all its hideous
harlequinade. Indeed, there can be little doubt that
Mr. Coates, with his vile performances, must be
held responsible for the decline of dramatic art in
England and the invasion of the amateur. The sight
of such folly, strutting unabashed, spoilt the prestige

of the theatre. To-day our stage is filled with tailors'-dummy heroes, with heroines who have real curls and can open and shut their eyes and, at a pinch, say 'mamma' and 'papa.' We must blame the Antiguan, I fear, for their existence. It was he —the rascal—who first spread that *scenæ sacra fames*. Some say that he was a schemer and impostor, feigning eccentricity for his private ends. They are quite wrong ; Mr. Coates was a very good man. He never made a penny out of his performances ; he even lost many hundred pounds. Moreover, as his speeches before the curtain and his letters to the papers show, he took himself quite seriously. Only the insane take themselves quite seriously.

It was the unkindness of his love that maddened him. But he lived to be the lightest-hearted of lunatics and caused great amusement for many years. Whether we think of him in his relation to history or psychology, dandiacal or dramatic art, he is a salient, pathetic figure. That he is memorable for his defects, not for his qualities, I know. But Romeo, in the tragedy of his wild love and frail intellect, in the folly that stretched the corners of his ' peculiar grin ' and shone in his diamonds and was emblazoned upon his tumbril,

145   K

is more suggestive than some sages.   He was so fantastic
an animal that Oblivion were indeed amiss.   If no
more, he was a great Fool.   In any case, it would be
fun to have seen him.

London, 1896.

DIMINUENDO

In the year of grace 1890, and in the beautiful autumn of that year, I was a freshman at Oxford. I remember how my tutor asked me what lectures I wished to attend, and how he laughed when I said that I wished to attend the lectures of Mr. Walter Pater. Also I remember how, one morning soon after, I went into Ryman's to order some foolish engraving for my room, and there saw, peering into a portfolio, a small, thick, rock-faced man, whose top-hat and gloves of *bright* dog-skin struck one of the many discords in that little city of learning or laughter. The serried bristles of his moustachio made for him a false-military air. I think I nearly went down when they told me that this was Pater.

Not that even in those more decadent days of my childhood did I admire the man as a stylist. Even

149

then I was angry that he should treat English as a dead language, bored by that sedulous ritual wherewith he laid out every sentence as in a shroud—hanging, like a widower, long over its marmoreal beauty or ever he could lay it at length in his book, its sepulchre. From that laden air, the so cadaverous murmur of that sanctuary, I would hook it at the beck of any jade. The writing of Pater had never, indeed, appealed to me, ἀλλ' αἰεί, having regard to the couth solemnity of his mind, to his philosophy, his rare erudition, τινα φῶτα μέγαν καὶ καλὸν ἐδέγμην. And I suppose it was when at length I saw him that I first knew him to be fallible.

At school I had read *Marius the Epicurean* in bed and with a dark lantern.   Indeed, I regarded it mainly as a tale of adventure, quite as fascinating as *Midshipman Easy*, and far less hard to understand, because there were no nautical terms in it.   Marryat, moreover, never made me wish to run away to sea, whilst certainly Pater did make me wish for more ' colour ' in the curriculum, for a renaissance of the Farrar period, when there was always ' a sullen spirit of revolt against the authorities '; when lockers were always being broken into and marks falsified, and small boys prevented from saying their prayers, insomuch that they vowed they would no longer buy brandy for their seniors. In some schools, I am told, the pretty old custom of roasting a fourth-form boy, whole, upon Founder's Day still survives. But in my school there was less sentiment. I ended by acquiescing in the slow revolution of its wheel of work and play. I felt that at Oxford, when I should be of age to matriculate, a 'variegated dramatic life' was waiting for me. I was not a little too sanguine, alas!

How sad was my coming to the university! Where were those sweet conditions I had pictured in my boyhood? Those antique contrasts? Did I ride, one sunset, through fens on a palfrey, watching the gold reflections on Magdalen Tower? Did I ride over Magdalen Bridge and hear the consonance of evening-bells and cries from the river below? Did I rein in to wonder at the raised gates of Queen's, the twisted pillars of St. Mary's, the little shops, lighted with tapers? Did bull-pups snarl at me, or dons, with bent backs, acknowledge my salute? Any one who knows the place as it is, must see that such questions are purely rhetorical. To him I need not explain the disappointment that beset me when, after being whirled in a cab from the station to a big hotel, I wandered out into the streets. *On aurait dit* a bit of Manchester through which Apollo had once passed ; for here, among the hideous trams and the brand-new bricks—here, glared at by the electric-lights that hung from poles, screamed at by boys with the *Echo* and the *Star*—here, in a riot of vulgarity, were remnants of beauty, as I discerned. There were only remnants.

Soon also I found that the life of the place, like the place, had lost its charm and its tradition. Gone were the contrasts that made it wonderful. That feud between undergraduates and dons—latent, in the old days, only at times when it behoved the two academic grades to unite against the townspeople—was one of the absurdities of the past. The townspeople now looked just like undergraduates and the dons just like townspeople. So splendid was the train-service between Oxford and London that, with hundreds of passengers daily, the one had become little better than a suburb of the other. What more could extensionists demand ? As for me, I was disheartened. Bitter were the comparisons I drew between my coming to Oxford and the coming of Marius to Rome. Could it be that there was at length no beautiful environment wherein a man

might sound the harmonies of his soul ? Had civilisation made beauty, besides adventure, so rare ? I
wondered what counsel Pater, insistent always upon
contact with comely things, would offer to one who
could nowhere find them. I had been wondering
that very day when I went into Ryman's and saw him
there.

When the tumult of my disillusioning was past, my
mind grew clearer. I discerned that the scope of my
quest for emotion must be narrowed. That abandon-
ment of one's self to life, that merging of one's soul in
bright waters, so often suggested in Pater's writing,
were a counsel impossible for to-day. The quest of
emotions must be no less keen, certainly, but the
manner of it must be changed forthwith. To unswitch
myself from my surroundings, to guard my soul from
contact with the unlovely things that compassed it
about, therein lay my hope. I must approach the
Benign Mother with great caution. And so, while
most of the freshmen were doing her honour with
wine and song and wreaths of smoke, I stood aside,
pondered. In such seclusion I passed my first term—
ah, how often did I wonder whether I was not wasting
my days, and, wondering, abandon my meditations

upon the right ordering of the future ! Thanks be to
Athene, who threw her shadow over me in those
moments of weak folly !

At the end of term I came to London. Around me
seethed swirls, eddies, torrents, violent cross-currents
of human activity. What uproar ! Surely I could
have no part in modern life. Yet, yet for a while it
was fascinating to watch the ways of its children. The
prodigious life of the Prince of Wales fascinated me
above all ; indeed, it still fascinates me. What
experience has been withheld from His Royal Highness ? Was ever so supernal a type, as he, of mere
Pleasure ? How often he has watched, at Newmarket,
the scud-a-run of quivering homuncules over the vert
on horses, or, from some night-boat, the holocaust of
great wharves by the side of the Thames ; raced
through the blue Solent ; threaded *les coulisses !* He
has danced in every palace of every capital, played in
every club. He has hunted elephants through the
jungles of India, boar through the forests of Austria,
pigs over the plains of Massachusetts. From the Castle
of Abergeldie he has led his Princess into the frosty
night, Highlanders lighting with torches the path to
the deer-larder, where lay the wild things that had

fallen to him on the crags. He has marched the
Grenadiers to chapel through the white streets of
Windsor. He has ridden through Moscow, in strange
apparel, to kiss the catafalque of more than one Tzar.
For him the Rajahs of India have spoiled their temples,
and Blondin has crossed Niagara along the tight-rope,
and the Giant Guard done drill beneath the chande-
liers of the Neue Schloss. Incline he to scandal,
lawyers are proud to whisper their secrets in his ear.
Be he gallant, the ladies are at his feet. *Ennuyé*, all
the wits from Bernal Osborne to Arthur Roberts have
jested for him. He has been 'present always at the
focus where the greatest number of forces unite in
their purest energy,' for it is his presence that makes
those forces unite.

'*Ennuyé ?*' I asked. Indeed he never is. How
could he be when Pleasure hangs constantly upon his
arm ! It is those others, overtaking her only after
arduous chase, breathless and footsore, who quickly
sicken of her company, and fall fainting at her feet.
And for me, shod neither with rank nor riches, what
folly to join the chase ! I began to see how small
a thing it were to sacrifice those external 'experiences,'
so dear to the heart of Pater, by a rigid, complex

civilisation made so hard to gain. They gave nothing
but lassitude to those who had gained them through
suffering. Even to the kings and princes, who so
easily gained them, what did they yield besides themselves? I do not suppose that, if we were invited to
give authenticated instances of intelligence on the part
of our royal pets, we could fill half a column of the
Spectator. In fact, their lives are so full they have no
time for thought, the highest energy of man. Now,
it was to thought that *my* life should be dedicated.
Action, apart from its absorption of time, would war
otherwise against the pleasures of intellect, which,
for me, meant mainly the pleasures of imagination.
It is only (this is a platitude) the things one has
not done, the faces or places one has not seen,
or seen but darkly, that have charm. It is only
mystery—such mystery as besets the eyes of children
—that makes things superb. I thought of the voluptuaries I had known — they seemed so sad, so
ascetic almost, like poor pilgrims, raising their eyes
never or ever gazing at the moon of tarnished
endeavour. I thought of the round, insouciant faces
of the monks at whose monastery I once broke bread,
and how their eyes sparkled when they asked me of

the France that lay around their walls. I thought, *pardie*, of the lurid verses written by young men who, in real life, know no haunt more lurid than a literary public-house. It was, for me, merely a problem how I could best avoid 'sensations,' 'pulsations,' and 'exquisite moments' that were not purely intellectual. I would not attempt to combine both kinds, as Pater seemed to fancy a man might. I would make myself master of some small area of physical life, a life of quiet, monotonous simplicity, exempt from all outer disturbance. I would shield my body from the world that my mind might range over it, not hurt nor fettered. As yet, however, I was in my first year at Oxford. There were many reasons that I should stay there and take my degree, reasons that I did not combat. Indeed, I was content to wait for my life.

And now that I have made my adieux to the Benign Mother, I need wait no longer. I have been casting my eye over the suburbs of London. I have taken a most pleasant little villa in ——ham, and here I shall make my home. Here there is no traffic, no harvest. Those of the inhabitants who do anything go away each morning and do it elsewhere. Here no vital forces unite. Nothing happens here. The days and the months will pass by me, bringing their sure recurrence of quiet events. In the spring-time I shall look out from my window and see the laburnum flowering in the little front garden. In summer cool syrups will come for me from the grocer's shop. Autumn will make the boughs of my mountain-ash scarlet, and, later, the asbestos in my grate will put forth its blossoms of flame. The infrequent cart of Buszard or Mudie will pass my window at all seasons. Nor will this be all. I shall have friends. Next door, there is a retired military man who has offered, in a most neighbourly way, to lend me his copy of the *Times*. On the other side of my house lives a charming family, who perhaps will call on me, now and again. I have seen them sally forth, at sundown, to catch the theatre-train ; among them walked a young lady, the charm of whose figure was ill concealed by the neat waterproof that overspread her evening dress. Some day it may be . . . but I anticipate. These things will be but the cosy accompaniment of my days. For I shall contemplate the world.

I shall look forth from my window, the laburnum and the mountain-ash becoming mere silhouettes in the foreground of my vision. I shall look forth and, in my remoteness, appreciate the distant pageant of the world. Humanity will range itself in the columns of my morning paper. No pulse of life will escape me. The strife of politics, the intriguing of courts, the wreck of great vessels, wars, dramas, earthquakes, national griefs or joys ; the strange sequels to divorces, even, and the mysterious suicides of land-agents at Ipswich—in all such phenomena I shall steep my exhaurient mind. *Delicias quoque bibliothecae experiar.* Tragedy, comedy, chivalry, philosophy will be mine. I shall listen to their music perpetually and their colours will dance before my eyes. I shall soar from terraces of stone upon dragons with shining wings and make war upon Olympus. From the peaks of hills I shall swoop into recondite valleys and drive the pigmies, shrieking little curses, to their caverns. It may be my whim to wander through infinite parks where the deer lie under the clustering shadow of their antlers and flee lightly over the grass ; to whisper with white prophets under the elms or bind a child with a daisy-chain or, with a lady, thread my way through the acacias. I shall swim down rivers into the sea and outstrip all ships. Unhindered I shall penetrate all sanctuaries and snatch the secrets of every dim confessional.

Yes ! among books that charm, and give wings to
the mind, will my days be spent. I shall be ever
absorbing the things great men have written ; with
such experience I will charge my mind to the full.
Nor will I try to give anything in return. Once, in the
delusion that Art, loving the recluse, would make his
life happy, I wrote a little for a yellow quarterly and
had that *succès de fiasco* which is always given to a young
writer of talent. But the stress of creation soon over-
whelmed me. Only Art with a capital H gives any
consolations to her henchmen. And I, who crave no
knighthood, shall write no more. I shall write no
more. Already I feel myself to be a trifle outmoded.
I belong to the Beardsley period. Younger men, with
months of activity before them, with fresher schemes
and notions, with newer enthusiasm, have pressed forward since then. *Cedo junioribus.* Indeed, I stand
aside with no regret. For to be outmoded is to be a
classic, if one has written well. I have acceded to the
hierarchy of good scribes and rather like my niche.

Chicago, 1895.

THE WORKS OF MAX BEERBOHM

A BIBLIOGRAPHY

BY

JOHN LANE

PREFACE

AFTER some considerable experience in the field of bibliography I cannot plead as palliation for any imperfections that may be discovered in this, that it is the work of a 'prentice hand. Difficult as I found my self-imposed task in the case of the Meredith and Hardy bibliographies, here my labour has been still more herculean.

It is impossible for one to compile a bibliography of a great man's works without making it in some sense a biography—and indeed, in the minds of not a few people, I have found a delusion that the one is identical with the other.

Mr. Beerbohm, as will be seen from the page headed *Personalia*, was born in London, August 24, 1872. In searching the files of the *Times* I naturally looked for other remarkable occurrences on that date.

There was only one worth recording. On the day upon which Mr. Beerbohm was born, there appeared in the first column of the *Times*, this announcement :

'On [Wednesday], the 21st August, at Brighton, the wife of V. P. Beardsley, Esq., of a son.'

That the same week should have seen the advent in this world of two such notable reformers as Aubrey Beardsley and Max Beerbohm is a coincidence to which no antiquary has previously drawn attention. Is it possible to over-estimate the influence of these two men in the art and literature of the century ?

Like two other great essayists, Addison and Steele, Mr. Beerbohm was educated at Charterhouse, and, like the latter, at Merton College, Oxford. At Charterhouse he is still remembered for his Latin verses, and for the superb gallery of portraits of the masters that he completed during his five years' sojourn there. There are still extant a few copies of his satire, in Latin elegiacs, called *Beccerius*, privately printed at the suggestion of Mr. A. H. Tod, his form-master. The writer has said 'Let it lie,' however, and in such a matter the author's wish should surely be regarded. I have myself been unable to obtain a sight of a copy, but a more fortunate friend has furnished me with a

careful description of the opusculum, which I print in
its place in the bibliography.

He matriculated at Merton in 1890, and immediately
applied himself to the task he had set before him,
namely, a gallery of portraits of the Dons.

I am aware that he contributed to *The Clown* and
other undergraduate journals : also that he was a
member of the Myrmidons' Club. It was during his
residence at Oxford that his famous treatise on
Cosmetics appeared in the pages of an important
London Quarterly, sets of which are still occasionally
to be found in booksellers' catalogues at a high price,
though the American millionaire collector has made it
one of the rarest of finds. These were the days of his
youth, the golden age of 'decadence.' For is not
decadence merely a *fin de siècle* literary term synonymous
with the 'sowing his wild oats' of our grandfathers ?
a phrase still surviving in agricultural districts, according to Mr. Andrew Lang, Mr. Edward Clodd,
and other Folk-Lorists.

Mr. Beerbohm, of course, was not the only writer
of his period who appeared as the champion of
artifice. A contemporary, one Richard Le Gallienne,
an eminent Pose Fancier, has committed himself

somewhere to the statement that 'The bravest men that ever trod this planet have worn corsets.'

But what is so far away as yester-year? In 1894, Mr. Beerbohm, in virtue of his 'Defence of Cosmetics,' was but a pamphleteer. In 1895 he was the famous historian, for in that year appeared the two earliest of his profound historical studies, The History of the Year 1880, and his work on King George the Fourth. During the growth of these masterpieces, his was a familiar figure in the British Museum and the Record Office, and tradition asserts that the enlargement of the latter building, which took place some time shortly afterwards, was mainly owing to his exertions.

Attended by his half-brother, Mr. Tree, Mrs. Tree and a numerous theatrical suite, he sailed on the 16th of January 1895, for America, with a view, it is said, to establishing a monarchy in that land. Mr. Beerbohm does not appear to have succeeded in this project, though he was interviewed in many of the newspapers of the States. He returned, *re infecta*, to the land of his birth, three months later.

After that he devoted himself to the completion of his life-work, here set forth.

The materials for this collection were drawn, with

the courteous acquiescence of various publishers, from *The Pageant*, *The Savoy*, *The Chap Book*, and *The Yellow Book*. Internal evidence shows that Mr. Beerbohm took fragments of his writings from *Vanity* (of New York) and *The Unicorn*, that he might inlay them in the First Essay, of whose scheme they are really a part. The Third Essay he re-wrote. The rest he carefully revised, and to some he gave new names.

Although it was my privilege on one occasion to meet Mr. Beerbohm—at five-o'clock tea—when advancing years, powerless to rob him of one shade of his wonderful urbanity, had nevertheless imprinted evidence of their flight in the pathetic stoop, and the low melancholy voice of one who, though resigned, yet yearns for the happier past, I feel that too precise a description of his personal appearance would savour of impertinence. The curious, on this point, I must refer to Mr. Sickert's and Mr. Rothenstein's portraits, which I hear that Mr. Lionel Cust is desirous of acquiring for the National Portrait Gallery.

It is needless to say that this bibliography has been a labour of love, and that any further information readers may care to send me will be gladly incorporated in future editions.

167

PREFACE

I must here express my indebtedness to Dr. Garnett, C.B., Mr. Bernard Quaritch, Mr. Clement K. Shorter, Mr. L. F. Austin, Mr. J. M. Bullock, Mr. Lewis Hind, Mr. and Mrs. H. Beerbohm Tree, Mrs. Leverson, and Miss Grace Conover, without whose assistance my work would have been far more arduous.

J. L.

THE ALBANY, *May 1896.*

THE BIBLIOGRAPHY

WORKS OF MAX BEERBOHM

1886.

A Letter to the Editor. *The Carthusian,* Dec. 1886, signed Diogenes.

A bitter cry of complaint against the dulness of the school paper. [Not reprinted.

[1890.]

Beccerius | a Latin fragment | with explanatory notes by M.B. [N.D.

About twelve couplets printed on rough yellow paper, pp. 1 to 4, cr. 8vo, notes in double columns at foot of page.

No publisher's or printer's name.

1894.

A Defence of Cosmetics. *The Yellow Book*, Vol. I., April 1894, pp. 65–82.

    Reprinted in 'The Works' under the title of 'The Pervasion of Rouge.'

Lines suggested by Miss Cissy Loftus. *The Sketch*, May 9, 1894, p. 71. A Caricature. [Not reprinted.

Mr. Phil May and Mr. Aubrey Beardsley. *The Pall Mall Budget*, June 7, 1894. Two Caricatures.

                        [Not reprinted.

Two Eminent Statesmen (the Rt. Hon. A. J. Balfour and the Rt. Hon. Sir Wm. Harcourt). *Pall Mall Budget*, July 5, 1894. Two Caricatures.

                        [Not reprinted.

Two Eminent Actors (Mr. Beerbohm Tree and Mr. Edward Terry). *Pall Mall Budget*, July 26, 1894. Two Caricatures.   [Not reprinted.

A Letter to the Editor. *The Yellow Book*, Vol. II., July 1894, pp. 281–284.   [Not reprinted.

1894.

Personal Remarks : Gus Elen (Caricature). *Pick-Me-Up*, Sept. 15, 1894. [Not reprinted.

Personal Remarks : Oscar Wilde (Caricature). *Pick-Me-Up*, Sept. 22, 1894. [Not reprinted.

Personal Remarks : R. G. Knowles, ' *There's a picture for you !* ' (Caricature). *Pick-Me-Up*, Sept. 29, 1894. [Not reprinted.

M. Henri Rochefort and Mr. Arthur Roberts. *Pall Mall Budget*, Oct. 4, 1894. Two Caricatures.
[Not reprinted.

Personal Remarks : Henry Arthur Jones (Caricature). *Pick-Me-Up*, Oct. 6, 1894. [Not reprinted.

Personal Remarks : Harry Furniss (Caricature). *Pick-Me-Up*, Oct. 13, 1894. [Not reprinted.

A Caricature of George the Fourth. *The Yellow Book*, Vol. III., Oct. 1894. [Not reprinted.

1894.

A Note on George the Fourth. *The Yellow Book*, Vol. III., Oct. 1894, pp. 247–269.

Reprinted in 'The Works' under the title of 'King George the Fourth.'

A parody of this appeared under the title of 'A Phalse Note on George the Fourth,' in *Punch*, October 27, 1894, p. 204.

Personal Remarks : Lord Lonsdale (Caricature). *Pick-Me-Up*, Oct 20, 1894.   [Not reprinted.

Personal Remarks : W. S. Gilbert (Caricature). *Pick-Me-Up*, Oct. 27, 1894.   [Not reprinted.

Personal Remarks : L. Raven Hill (Caricature). *Pick-Me-Up*, Nov. 3, 1894.   [Not reprinted.

Personal Remarks : The Marquis of Queensberry (Caricature). *Pick-Me-Up*, Nov. 17, 1894.

[Not reprinted.

Personal Remarks : Ada Reeve (Caricature). *Pick-Me-Up*, Nov. 24, 1894.   [Not reprinted.

Personal Remarks : Seymour Hicks (Caricature). *Pick-Me-Up*, Dec. 1, 1894.   [Not reprinted.

1894.

Personal Remarks : Corney Grain (Caricature). *Pick-Me-Up*, Dec. 8, 1894. [Not reprinted.

Personal Remarks : Lord Randolph Churchill (Caricature). *Pick-Me-Up*, Dec. 22, 1894.

[Not reprinted.

Personal Remarks : Dutch Daly (Caricature). *Pick-Me-Up*, Dec. 29, 1894. [Not reprinted.

1895.

Character Sketches of 'The Chieftain' at the Savoy.
    i. Mr. Courtice Pounds.
    ii. Mr. Scott Fishe.
    iii. Mr. Walter Passmore.
Pick-Me-Up, Jan. 5, 1895.   ·   [Not reprinted.

Personal Remarks : Henry Irving (Caricature). *Pick-Me-Up*, Jan. 5, 1895.

' 1880.' *The Yellow Book*, Vol. IV., Jan. 1895, pp. 275–283. Reprinted in ' The Works.'

    A parody of this appeared, under the title of ' 1894,' by Max Mereboom, in *Punch*, February 2, 1895, p. 58.

1895.

Character Sketches of 'An Ideal Husband' at the Haymarket.

    i. Mr. Bishop.
    ii. Mr. Charles Hawtrey.
    iii. Miss Julia Neilson.

Pick-Me-Up, Jan. 19, 1895.   [Not reprinted.

Personal Remarks : Harry Marks (Caricature). *Pick-Me-Up*, Jan. 19, 1895.   [Not reprinted.

Personal Remarks : F. C. Burnand (Caricature). *Pick-Me-Up*, Jan. 26, 1895.   [Not reprinted.

Dandies and Dandies. *Vanity* (New York). Feb. 7, 1895.

    The above has been reprinted with additions and alterations in 'The Works.'

Personal Remarks : Arthur Pinero (Caricature). *Pick-Me-Up*, Feb. 9, 1895.   [Not reprinted.

Dandies and Dandies. *Vanity* (New York). Feb. 14, 1895.

1895.

Dandies and Dandies. *Vanity* (New York). Feb. 21, 1895.

The above have been reprinted with additions and alterations in ' The Works.'

Personal Remarks : The Rt. Hon. Sir William Vernon Harcourt (Caricature). *Pick-Me-Up*, Feb. 23, 1895.
[Not reprinted.

Dandies and Dandies. *Vanity* (New York). Feb. 28, 1895.

The above has been reprinted with additions and alterations in ' The Works.'

Personal Remarks : Earl Spencer (Caricature). *Pick-Me-Up*, March 9, 1895. [Not reprinted.

Personal Remarks : Arthur Balfour (Caricature). *Pick-Me-Up*, March 16, 1895. [Not reprinted.

Personal Remarks : S. B. Bancroft (Caricature). *Pick-Me-Up*, March 23, 1895. [Not reprinted.

Personal Remarks : Paderewski (Caricature). *Pick-Me-Up*, March 30, 1895. [Not reprinted.

Personal Remarks : Colonel North (Caricature). *Pick-Me-Up*, April 6, 1895. [Not reprinted.

1895.

Personal Remarks : Alfred de Rothschild. *Pick-Me-Up*, April 20, 1895.   [Not reprinted.

Merton. (The Warden of Merton.) *The Octopus*, May 25, 1895. A Caricature.   [Not reprinted.

Seen on the Towpath. *The Octopus*, May 29, 1895. A Caricature.   [Not reprinted.

An Evening of Peculiar Delirium. *The Sketch*, July 24, 1895.   [Not reprinted.

Notes in Foppery. *The Unicorn*, Sept. 18, 1895.

Notes in Foppery. *The Unicorn*, Sept. 25, 1895.

> The above have been reprinted with additions and alterations in ' The Works,' under the title of ' Dandies and Dandies.'

Press Notices on ' Punch and Judy,' selected by Max Beerbohm. *The Sketch*, Oct. 16, 1895 (p. 644).
                    [Not reprinted.

Be it Cosiness. *The Pageant*, Christmas, 1895, pp. 230-235.

1895.

Reprinted in 'The Works' under the title of 'Diminuendo.'

A parody of this appeared, under the title of 'Be it Cosiness,' by Max Mereboom, in *Punch*, Dec. 21, 1895, p. 297.

1896.

A Caricature of Mr. Beerbohm Tree, a wood engraving after the drawing by Max Beerbohm. *The Savoy*, No. 1, Jan. 1896, p. 125.　　　　[Not reprinted.

A Good Prince. *The Savoy*, No. 1, Jan. 1896, pp. 45–7.　　　　[Reprinted in 'The Works.'

De Natura Barbatulorum. *The Chap-Book*, Feb. 15, 1896, pp. 305–312.

The above has been reprinted with additions and alterations in 'The Works,' under the title of 'Dandies and Dandies.'

Poor Romeo ! *The Yellow Book*, Vol. IX., April '96, pp. 169–181.　　　　[Reprinted in 'The Works.'

1896.

A Caricature of Aubrey Beardsley. A wood engraving after the drawing by Max Beerbohm. *The Savoy*, No. 2, April 1896, p. 161.

PERSONALIA.

On the 24th instant, at 57 Palace Gardens Terrace, Kensington, the wife of J. E. Beerbohm, Esq., of a son. *The Times*, Aug. 26, 1872.

A few words with Mr. Max Beerbohm. (An interview by Ada Leverson.) *The Sketch*, Jan. 2, 1895, p. 439.

Max Beerbohm : an interview by Isabel Brooke Alder. *Woman*, April 29, 1896, pp. 8 & 9.

On Mr. Beerbohm leaving Oxford in July 1895, he took up his residence at 19 Hyde Park Place, formerly the residence of another well-known historian— W. C. Kinglake. *Woman*, April 29, 1896, p. 8.

PORTRAITS OF MR. MAX BEERBOHM.

Max Beerbohm in ' Boyhood.' *The Sketch*, Jan. 2, 1895, p. 439.

178

BIBLIOGRAPHY

Max Beerbohm. *Oxford Characters.* Lithographs by
Will Rothenstein. Part 6.
It is believed this artist did several pastels of Mr.
Beerbohm.

Portrait of Mr. Beerbohm standing before a picture of
George the Fourth, by Walter Sickert.

Mr. Max Beerbohm. *Woman,* April 29, 1896, p. 8.